Education, Philosophy and the Ethical Environment

D1170294

The Foundations and Futures of Education series focuses on key emerging issues in education as well as continuing debates within the field. The series is interdisciplinary and includes historical, philosophical, sociological, psychological and comparative perspectives on three major themes: the purposes and nature of education; increasing interdisciplinarity within the subject; and the theory–practice divide.

Around the world there is concern about the climate of values in which young people are growing up. Liberal ideas about personal morality and the importance of individual choice are spreading worldwide but often meeting resistance from more traditional values. Everywhere, people look to education to promote the values they believe to be right and to help ward off perceived threats to these values. But how much can we reasonably expect of education?

This book, written by a philosopher of education, casts new light on that question by seeing values education, not as a separate activity within schools, but as an aspect of education that both reflects the surrounding climate of values and can help to change it. Graham Haydon argues that all of us – whether as teachers, parents, students or citizens – share in a responsibility for the quality of that ethical environment.

We must ensure that what happens in schools will:

- enable young people to appreciate the diversity of our ethical environment
- help them find their way through its complexities
- contribute to developing a climate of values that is desirable for all.

This book shows that values education is too demanding to be left to parents and too important to be entrusted to government initiatives. For teachers engaged in values education – including those teaching citizenship, personal and social education, or religious education – this book brings a fresh perspective to what they are doing, within a realistic view of their responsibilities. For students of education it shows that practical issues can be illuminated by insights from philosophy.

Graham Haydon is Senior Lecturer in Philosophy of Education, Institute of Education, University of London, UK.

Foundations and Futures of Education
Edited by Peter Aggleton, David Halpin and Sally Power

Education and the Family
Passing success across the generations
Leon Feinstein, Kathryn Duckworth and Ricardo Sabates

Educational Activity and the Psychology of Learning
Judith Ireson

Improving Schools
Using research to inform practice
Frank McNeil and Pamela Sammons

Schooling, Society and Curriculum
Alex Moore

Gender, Schooling and Social Justice
Elaine Unterhalter

Education, Philosophy and the Ethical Environment

Graham Haydon

Routledge
Taylor & Francis Group

LONDON AND NEW YORK

First published 2006 by Routledge
2 Park Square, Milton Park, Abingdon, Oxon OX14 4RN

Simultaneously published in the USA and Canada
by Routledge
270 Madison Ave, New York, NY 10016

*Routledge is an imprint of the Taylor & Francis Group,
an informa business*

© 2006 Graham Haydon

Typeset in Galliard by
RefineCatch Limited, Bungay, Suffolk
Printed and bound in Great Britain by
MPG Books Ltd, Bodmin

British Library Cataloguing in Publication Data
A catalogue record for this book is available from the British Library

Library of Congress Cataloging in Publication Data
A catalog record for this book has been requested

ISBN10: 0–415–35661–X (hbk)
ISBN10: 0–415–35662–8 (pbk)
ISBN10: 0–203–00270–9 (ebk)

ISBN13: 978–0–415–35661–9 (hbk)
ISBN13: 978–0–415–35662–6 (pbk)
ISBN13: 978–0–203–00270–4 (ebk)

In memory of
Terence H. McLaughlin

Contents

Series editors' foreword

One of the most remarkable shifts within societies over the last 200 years has been the universal development of mass education. With each successive decade, provision has expanded to encompass more learners at more stages in their lives. The ambitions for education systems have also expanded to encompass objectives as diverse as personal fulfilment and wellbeing, cultural transmission, active citizenship, social cohesion and, increasingly, international economic competitiveness. The broad range of ambitions and the sheer pace of change have created a climate in which it is difficult to stand back and make sense of what education is for and where it should be going. *Foundations and Futures of Education* provides an opportunity to engage with these fundamental issues in new and exciting ways.

The series adopts a broad and interdisciplinary stance, including historical, philosophical, sociological, psychological and comparative approaches as well as those derived from work within the fields of media and cultural studies. It also reflects the wider conception of education that is embedded in concepts such as 'the knowledge economy', 'the learning society' and 'lifelong learning'.

The academic rigour of the arguments is balanced with accessible writing which we hope will engage the interest of those working in and for education, as well as a wide range of undergraduate and postgraduate students. Although it will be clear that there are few 'easy answers' to the questions raised, we hope that you will find the debates and dialogues exciting and thought-provoking.

Education, Philosophy and the Ethical Environment raises important issues for all of those who are concerned with the relationship between education and values. One of the key debates in recent years has been the role of schools in developing socially responsible citizens. At various moments moral panics emerge about student behaviour and perceived indiscipline within schools. On other occasions, concerns are voiced that the concentration on academic standards has squeezed out teaching students about other values which contribute to social and personal wellbeing. However, in most of these debates, the focus is on how the curriculum might be changed or what new subjects should be added to the timetable. Attention is rarely given to the climate in which such educational activities take place.

As Graham Haydon points out, although we now have increased awareness of the importance of the physical environment, we rarely consider the *ethical* environment in which we live and work. This is something which merits serious consideration. As Haydon rightly argues, 'Education is important to the quality of the ethical environment; and the ethical environment has an important bearing on the nature and quality of education at a particular time and place.'

Through concentrating on the ethical climate in which children learn, Graham Haydon unravels in a clear and insightful way some of the issues which need to be addressed. These involve clarification of the nature and purpose of education, of the nature and purpose of values education and of how education and values can be brought into an appropriate relationship with each other within an ethical environment.

Finally, but by no means least important, this book realises one of the key aims of this series in showcasing the considerable value of foundational thinking. Its timely appearance, its clear and lively thinking and the fundamental questions that it raises should certainly dispel any notion that philosophical enquiry is dry, irrelevant or indulgent. Without serious attention to the kind of analysis presented in this book our educational policies and practices will be unfocused and ineffective.

Peter Aggleton, Thomas Coram Research Unit, Institute of Education, UK
David Halpin, Thomas Coram Research Unit, Institute of Education, UK
Sally Power, University of Cardiff, UK

Acknowledgements

It would be paradoxical and self-defeating to claim that the ideas in a book about the ethical environment have their origins in my own head. I shall be drawing attention throughout to ideas that are already part of that environment; many of them have been discussed, though often in a different context, within recent philosophy of education and moral philosophy. Often such ideas, as currents of thought, cannot be attributed to any single author, but the references will indicate many of the influences. I want here to acknowledge a specific stimulus to my own thinking provided by some paragraphs in Simon Blackburn's *Being Good*, which I take up in Chapter 1. I also want to thank all those who through their comments, questions and critiques over the years have contributed to the development of my thinking on the ethical environment (much of that thinking happened before I had identified the topic in its present form). These people are too numerous to list by name, but they certainly include many members of the research community in Philosophy of Education at the Institute of Education.

I have explicitly discussed the importance of the ethical environment for education in two previous publications. 'Values Education: sustaining the ethical environment' in *Journal of Moral Education*, 33, 2004 gives an overview of some of the arguments, and *The Importance of PSHE: A philosophical and policy perspective on Personal, Social and Health Education* (Philosophy of Education Society of Great Britain, 2005) applies some of the arguments to a specific issue in the English National Curriculum. The comments of anonymous readers of earlier drafts of those works, and of a first proposal for this book, have all helped me to improve the present work.

I owe some particular acknowledgements to students and colleagues. The editors of the *Foundations and Futures of Education* series, Peter Aggleton, David Halpin and Sally Power, have been supportive throughout. The members of my MA Values in Education class in the Spring term of 2005 – Steve Adler, Ellie Atkins, Yen-Hsin Chen, James Edleston, Simon Frost, Rukhsana

Haji, Mark Holmes, Spyros Loucaides and Alex Rowe – allowed me to try out on them many of the ideas in this book during the writing of the first draft, and contributed to it by their lively discussion. Terry McLaughlin took the time to read that first version closely and make detailed comments. I am grateful for all the points raised by readers of the earlier version, even when I have not managed to do justice to them. Responsibility for the opinions expressed in this book and for any mistakes in the claims made remains, of course, mine.

Introduction

In many parts of the world there is concern about the climate of values in which people live and in which young people grow up. Liberal ideas about personal morality and the value of individual choice are spreading worldwide, but not without resistance. Some would say they have already been taken to an extreme in much of Europe and North America. In all parts of the world, though perhaps in some countries more than others, liberal ideas are seen as being in tension with more traditional values. In some places and at some times the emphasis may be more on education doing what is best for each individual, at other times and places more on promoting what is best for society. Everywhere there seems to be an expectation that education will both promote whatever values are perceived as best and help to stem the encroaching tide of values that are seen as threatening.

The paragraph above sets out, in terms that are both too simple and too vague, the situation to which this book is a response. A convenient term is needed for those aspects of education with which this book is concerned. The best term available, I think, of those that have some currency already, is *values education*. But in using that term, I want it to be understood, especially at this early stage in the book, with as few preconceptions as possible. I do not want 'values education' at this stage to be equated with any particular conception of what it is about: of its aims, its content or its procedures. If, for instance, you think that values education is about producing good citizens, I would say that that is only one conception of the aims of values education, and one that is at best only partial. Or if you think values education is about *transmitting* values, or, alternatively, about enabling individuals to think for themselves about values, I would say that each of these ideas captures some aspects, but only some aspects, of values education. If you think values education is about morality, I would say that morality, while vital, by no means exhausts all the values that are important to us, so that *moral education* will be only one aspect of values education. If you think that values education should proceed through precepts and example, or through discussion and reflection, I would say there is a place for many approaches.

I also want to avoid preconceptions about the relationship between values education and the school curriculum. Perhaps there should be some distinct part of the curriculum that is called 'values education', or some equivalent title; perhaps values education should be seen, not as a compartment of the curriculum, like a specific subject, but as an aspect of *all* education, extending not merely across the whole curriculum but across all areas of school organisation and educational policy. Or perhaps it should be seen as an aspect of all education *and* have a part of the curriculum devoted to it.

We need first to take a broader look at the whole area of values and the relationship of education to values; then we can begin to be more specific about how we might reasonably understand values education. That is essentially what I hope to do in this book. In doing it I use a notion – a conceptual tool – that I think is helpful. That is the idea of the *ethical environment*. As a first approximation, what I called in the first line above 'the climate of values in which people live and in which young people grow up' is what I mean by 'the ethical environment', though I shall have to say much more about that idea. I am going to suggest that once we have the notion of the ethical environment in place, and an appreciation of the richness and diversity of that environment, then we can use it to give us a sense of the scope of values education, and a way of saying what it is that values education should be trying to do. I shall say that it is the task of values education both to nurture and sustain the ethical environment, and to help individuals to find their way through that environment. I intend this as a way of thinking about values education, a general orientation, that can be taken up in any country. I do not here go into the details of policy and practice in any specific country, since it is part of my argument that such details will always have to be worked out within the context of a specific ethical environment.

To see values education in this way requires a good deal of groundwork to be laid first. In the process, this book will serve as an introduction to a variety of ideas about values education, and to some of the relevant work within moral philosophy and political philosophy (we can say in advance that both are relevant, since values education has connections with both morality and citizenship). The references will indicate further reading through which many themes can be followed up. But this book will not be a neutral survey of the field, since in contrast with much of the academic literature on values education I shall not be concentrating on the development of beliefs or tendencies or capacities in individuals, but on the relevance of environmental factors.

The task for the first chapter will be to introduce the idea of the ethical environment more systematically. The task for the rest of this Introduction is to prepare the ground for the way that I shall approach the issues, since I am coming, not from sociology or from psychology, but from philosophy. Since I am not interested *only* in addressing people who have already decided that philosophy of education is for them, I need to say something about what my philosophical approach entails.

Philosophy and foundations

This book is a contribution to a multi-disciplinary series called *Foundations and Futures*. It is certainly about possible futures, because it raises questions about what kind of future we should hope to see, and about how education might help us to get to a desirable kind of future; more particularly, about the potential role of education in future in achieving and maintaining a desirable ethical environment. But to introduce the philosophical approach taken here it will be more helpful to start from the idea of *foundations*.

Philosophy has sometimes claimed a status as one of the 'foundation disciplines' of education. Philosophers have always challenged people to think about the foundations of their values and beliefs. Some philosophers have done this in a spirit of scepticism, suggesting that there are actually no foundations to be had: that we are deluded if we think there is some firm grounding for what we *think* we know about the way the world is and about the way we should behave. Other philosophers have not only believed that there are foundations but have, to their own satisfaction, confidently displayed the foundations. Here the challenge to everyday thinking consists at least in the claim to take a more systematic and coherent view than the everyday one, and often also in the fact that the foundations displayed may be quite at odds with the common sense of the day. What both forms of challenge, the sceptical and the confident, have in common is that anyone who takes them seriously cannot rest content in simply taking their own values and beliefs for granted.

When philosophers have written about education, it has often been in a spirit of confidence. If they can offer firm foundations – some fixed truths, say, about human nature and the nature of knowledge – then on these foundations they could erect an account of what education is about, and on that in turn could rest some prescriptions for the practical business of education.

It may be that some people still expect philosophy of education to offer foundations in that way. But in philosophy more generally there have been strong currents in the opposite direction through the last century and more. 'Anti-foundationalism' is a common theme. We inhabit webs of perceptions, languages, beliefs, values; and there is no way we can get outside of these to foundations on which they can be supported: some neutral ground from which we can survey them and assess them.

If philosophy is not offering foundations, does that mean that it has nothing to offer educational theory? It does not, because there is still the challenge to think about what basis we can have for confidence in our current practices. Here, even when philosophy has been anti-foundationalist, it has not always been pessimistic. Often instead it has said that it was a mistake all along to look for a basis for confidence outside our ongoing beliefs and practices. The practices that we share with other human beings give us the only basis for confidence that we can have, which is also the only one we need.

This emphatically does not mean that we should simply rest content with the practices and beliefs we currently have. These may be muddled, inconsistent, exclusive rather than inclusive, and in many other ways open to question and criticism. The criticism does not collapse just because it is not erected on some firm ground outside the whole of our webs of perceptions, languages, beliefs, values and practices. There are plenty of resources for criticism within those webs. This point will be very relevant later in the book when we ask how it is possible to be critical of the ethical environment in which we live.

Does the lack of foundations mean that questioning and criticism will be interminable, never finding any resting point? Yes, but why should we wish it otherwise for a practical activity like education? Educational practices that are unquestioned will surely at best become moribund, at worst turn out – at some future point when we have the benefit of hindsight – to have been going in some direction we regret.

What confidence we have, then, should be provisional, founded on the capacity of certain beliefs, values and practices to have stood up to criticism so far. Philosophy's challenge to us to think about what we are doing and why remains vital. Do we really understand what we are doing? Can we give good reasons for it? What if we don't understand, and can't give good reasons? To ask these questions is not to imply that something that is not fully understood, or that cannot be justified from first principles, is not worth doing. But it does rest on a belief – not itself beyond dispute – that on the whole we are likely to do what we are doing better if we understand what it is we are trying to do and why. I am writing this book in the faith that this holds true for values education.

Philosophy and methods

So far I have said something about the way in which philosophy can be about foundations, but nothing about how it actually proceeds. Other ways of studying education can talk about their methodologies, and may ask philosophy for an account of its own methods.

There is a lot that can be said about the methods of philosophy in general and of philosophy of education in particular. Part of what has to be said is that there are many kinds of philosophy and many ways of doing it. Since this is intended to be a philosophical book about education, not a book about the subject called philosophy of education, I shall only list a few of the things that philosophy (when it is not in a system-building mode) does.

Philosophy often asks us to think about the words that we use. How are we using these words? Why are we using one word rather than another? What distinctions are we intending to mark? Questions like these are certainly needed about educational discourse. Too much talk about education puts words together in familiar combinations that bypass serious reflection. 'Education' goes with 'school' and also today with 'skills' (as in the name of a current UK government department), 'accountability' goes with 'targets', 'values' goes with 'transmission', 'behaviour' goes with 'standards', 'tolerance' goes with 'respect', and so on. And an unreflective use of words often overlooks the possibility of distinctions that would be an aid to clarity; philosophy will often be careful to make distinctions, or to call attention to existing ones.

Philosophy looks for assumptions that may be hidden in ordinary discourse. 'If you are to hold this position, then (whether you realise it or not) you are presupposing that . . .'. Then other implications of the same presupposition may be deduced, or the presupposition itself may be challenged.

Philosophy scrutinises arguments for consistency. Is one position that someone holds actually compatible with another position that the same person also holds? Often, too, philosophy challenges a position by asking whether the person who holds it would also be willing to hold a consistent position about some other case that appears to be similar in relevant ways.

Philosophy makes arguments of its own, trying to start from an explicit basis and to move logically from one step to another. This is not necessarily system-building from first principles. The starting point may be one that is explicitly assumed for the purposes of a particular argument, since one cannot argue for everything at once. An argument may, for instance, start from an assumption that a good society is liberal and democratic, without denying that those assumptions can be criticised and defended in other places.

None of the moves in argument that I have mentioned here is exclusive to philosophy; any researcher or writer about education may do any of these things. But often in work that is not consciously philosophical these moves in argument are passed over quickly or almost unnoticed on the way to getting to what are seen as the important points. Philosophy wants to pause, to take time to reflect, to bring to the foreground what might otherwise be missed.

Philosophy holds, or should hold, its own assumptions and claims open to criticism and testing. What sort of criticism and testing that should be depends on the nature of the claims. Indeed philosophy often has to ask explicitly what kind of claim is being made both in its own arguments and those of other disciplines. There are many issues that could not be settled by any empirical method. These include the question from which we started above: are there foundations for our beliefs and values? There is no way this could be tested empirically, no possibility of designing a foundation-detector. Questions about whether we have got our values right are apparently of the same kind, though it is easy to miss the point and it is in any case more open to dispute. It may be possible (though not very straightforward) through surveys and interviews to establish facts about the values people hold, but it is not possible to establish by the same methods whether their values are right or misguided.

Nevertheless, though philosophy does not (usually) conduct experiments (other than thought-experiments) or interviews or surveys, it does have to pay attention to the way things are. A philosophical argument is rarely one that goes through by formal logic alone. Some sort of appeal to experience is necessary, especially when an attempt is made to say something worth saying about a practical matter. But if philosophy is making assumptions or claims about the way things are, without testing these, does it not fall by its own standards?

Philosophy does indeed often appeal to what it takes to be common experience and even common knowledge. Wittgenstein (1972: 31(para. 66)) once said in a specific context 'Don't think, but look'. Look and see how it is, rather than following an argument that suggests it must be a certain way. That is a useful warning against an over-reliance on philosophical argument, but it carries its own dangers. The results of our looking are themselves constrained within a framework of concepts and assumptions, which we cannot break out of by looking alone. (Does it *look* as if the earth goes round the sun?) Looking *and* thinking are needed. What philosophy often does is to ask people to reflect on their own experience and to see whether they agree that things are the way the philosopher suggests they are. As Leavis said of literary appraisal (Smith 1997: 111), so philosophy also often asks 'It is like this, isn't it?'

In asking this, philosophy is not necessarily conservative. Sometimes it will suggest that, after all, the answer to some problem is to be found by looking carefully at what we knew all along. At other times it will suggest that a new way of thinking will prove more fruitful. Looking at what is familiar from a different direction, perhaps using a different vocabulary, can give us new insights. This is part of what I hope to do in this book by using the vocabulary of 'the ethical environment'.

One way or another, then, philosophy – especially if it hopes to say something significant about a practical area like education – cannot go far without making claims about the way the world is. Where such claims *can* be tested in more rigorous ways, then they should be, but it is not necessarily the philosopher who should do this. There is a division of labour in the academic world as in the industrial. When a philosopher points out that a certain claim is an empirical one, open to testing, it may be other researchers who have the relevant experience and skills who do the testing.

Some may find philosophical writing about education frustrating in that it often seems to move at a certain level of abstraction, some way removed from concrete details about this or that educational practice. Others may find that it is just this degree of abstraction from the concrete that gives philosophy its capacity to reflect on and raise questions about what may often be taken for granted within current practice. Certainly within educational discourse both examination of detailed practice and reflection at the level of underlying principles are needed, and they should be seen as complementary. It is good that educational literature contains both kinds of writing, and that at least the larger academic institutions that engage in study and teaching about education should be able to accommodate a few philosophers.

Because it is complementary to other disciplines, philosophy of education should be wary of claims to authority. It can only be one voice among others in an ongoing discourse about education. But it is an important part of the discourse, not least – as new students of the subject often find – because it helps to create space within the discourse for reflection on the discourse itself. While philosophy in no way stands in opposition to empirical research on education, it does tend to be opposed to the predominance in modern educational discourse of technicist, instrumental ways of looking at educational practice – the ways that allow ends (targets, goals, objectives) to be taken for granted or created by fiat, while research is expected to find the ways and means for realising those ends. Philosophy asks for and helps to create the space in which the ends and values can be better understood and, if necessary, criticised. That is, above all, its foundational contribution to the practice of education.

Philosophy in this book

I have written of the challenge that philosophy always offers. But challenge in this sense does not have to be combative. I would prefer to see myself in this book as offering an invitation to engage in reflection. Ideally I would be engaging the reader in actual dialogue, but some aspects of dialogue can be approximated even on the printed page.

Dialogue is an exchange of views and a mutual exploration of those views. No voice in dialogue can claim overriding authority. An impersonal academic style may disguise this fact, by expressing views in the passive voice as if they were not the views of an individual expressing his or her thoughts. Within academic writing, philosophy more than many disciplines does allow the author's voice to be expressed ('I think', 'I shall argue', and so on). In this book I shall make some conscious accommodation to the impersonal style that is more usual within education as an academic discipline, speaking in the first person rather less after this Introduction and after the opening paragraphs of each chapter. Nevertheless, even when I do not say 'I think', I shall be expressing what I think, and the reader is hereby invited to agree or disagree.

A dialogue is not, however, simply a face-off of statements of different views. It is or should be a mutual exploration of views, and exploring a view involves seeing how far it can be defended. To say 'that's just your opinion' is to bring dialogue to an end, often before it has really started. I shall, I hope, be constantly offering reasons and arguments for what I say, and if you are persuaded by those reasons and arguments you will at least to some degree come to share my views. Not because they are *my* views, but because you will have seen that there are (in *your* view) good reasons and arguments for them.

Besides, the response 'that's just your opinion' is in a sense never true. If the ethical environment has the importance I think it has, then (as I have already indicated in the Acknowledgements) everything anyone says in a dialogue about values, including everything I say in this book, will be some sort of reflection of what is already available in that environment. Even if there were some authoritative position available outside of the ethical environment in which we live, I personally would be disinclined to claim it; but in any case there is no such position available.

Since many of the ideas I shall be discussing are part of a shared ethical environment, many of the references in this book will be to exemplifications of a point rather than to an unique source. Where one is aware of a specific source for an idea or for the way the idea is formulated then it is good manners, as well as often a requirement of intellectual property rights, to acknowledge it. But quotation and citation of sources should not be mistaken for appeals to authority, still less as giving solid foundations for claims. Other sources are themselves voices in a dialogue. Sometimes they are voices well informed through experience and empirical research, but that cannot make them final authorities. In fields such as educational research and social psychology, for all their relevance to the ideas in this book, there is always room for alternative interpretations and explanations. One pertinent warning to any students who may be reading this book as part of their preparation for assessed work would be: do not say 'research has *proved* that . . .'. A second warning would be: if you consider that I have said something interesting that is worth thinking about further, by all means quote me, but do not give your own readers the impression that you think something must be right because this book has said it.

Finally in this Introduction, an outline of the contents of the book. What is this *ethical environment* that I am talking about? That is the question which I address in the first chapter. In the second chapter I bring out how very diverse the nature of this ethical environment is – a diversity which I shall later argue it is important for us to hold on to. In the third chapter I turn more systematically to a number of ideas about the nature of values education, arguing both that these ideas are themselves part of our ethical environment, and that, on any of the conceptions reviewed, the success of values education depends on the nature of the surrounding ethical environment. I suggest that, taking a social perspective, we can see values education as a way of nurturing and sustaining our ethical environment, while its task at an individual level is to help people find their way through that environment. In Chapter 4 I argue that we should see our ethical environment, not as something independent of us over which we can have no control, but as something for which we can take a degree of responsibility. In the fifth chapter I ask whether it is legitimate for governments to seek to sustain or to change the ethical environment – an important question because (I believe) values education, often to be institutionalised in schools through state action, is an important way in which we can exercise our responsibility for the ethical environment. In Chapter 6 I give an overview of the tasks that face education in relation to the ethical environment; the questions to be considered are not only about the curriculum but also about the structure of public systems of schooling and about the internal environment of schools. Finally in the Conclusion I ask, if we are to take seriously the fact that education operates within an ethical environment which it also influences, what does this say about the responsibilities both of teachers and of governments?

1 The ethical environment

Since the idea of the ethical environment is going to figure largely in this book, I need to clarify it and anticipate some of the questions that may be raised about my use of the phrase. I am not proposing 'the ethical environment' as a technical term. Accordingly I shall not offer a definition of it, just as I did not offer a definition of 'values education' in the Introduction. While clarifying how you are using a term is generally a good idea in philosophy and indeed in other research, offering a definition in advance of discussion is often not the best route to clarification. Instead I shall start from the context in which I was first struck by the term and its potential, and from there work through a number of issues with the aim of constructing a conception of the ethical environment that will be useful in this book.

The idea of the ethical environment

Simon Blackburn's book *Being Good* (Blackburn 2001) is intended as a popular introduction to ethics (the terms 'ethics' and 'moral philosophy' are used more or less interchangeably as labels for a certain area of academic philosophy). In his opening paragraph he writes:

> We have all learned to become sensitive to the physical environment. We know that we depend upon it, that it is fragile, and that we have the power to ruin it, thereby ruining our own lives, or more probably those of our descendants. Perhaps fewer of us are sensitive to what we might call the moral or ethical environment. This is the surrounding climate of ideas about how to live. It determines what we find acceptable or unacceptable, admirable or contemptible. It determines our conception of when things are going well and when they are going badly. It determines our conception of what is due to us, and what is due from us, as we relate to others. It shapes our emotional responses, determining what is a

cause of pride or shame, or anger or gratitude, or what can be forgiven
and what cannot. It gives us our standards – our standards of behaviour.

Blackburn 2001: 1[1]

This is already enough to show the importance of the ethical environment.
But we need more attention to the idea before we can use it in thinking about
values education.

Blackburn glosses 'ethical environment' as 'the surrounding climate of
ideas about how to live'. He goes on in the next paragraph to point out that
'[t]he workings of the ethical environment can be strangely invisible' (2001:
2), since 'we may not be aware of our ideas' (Blackburn 2001: 3). This is a
good starting point for further exploration. We might wonder how we can be
unaware of our ideas. Where is an idea, if it is not in your head? How can you
have an idea, if you are not conscious of it?

The way that ideas exist and make a difference to us is more subtle than
that. For a start, even if a certain idea doesn't exist in your head, it may exist in
other people's heads, and that may affect the way they talk and behave, which
may in various ways affect you in turn. So the ideas that other people have can
be part of the ethical environment in which you live.

Second, ideas can certainly exist in a person's head without the person
being conscious of them at any particular time (if at all). Blackburn explains
that an idea 'in this sense is a tendency to accept routes of thought and feeling
that we may not recognise in ourselves, or even be able to articulate' (Blackburn 2001: 3). Such tendencies, then, are patterns in the way we respond to
the world. These patterns may be encoded physically in our bodies in some
way, within the nervous system and hormonal system; in that sense they may
be quite literally in your head. If you prefer to think of these tendencies as
being in your mind, and your mind as being something distinct from your
brain, that is unlikely to affect the arguments of this book, though it raises
difficult issues that other areas of philosophy have looked at. For the purposes
of the argument here it will sometimes be helpful to distinguish between
tendencies in our physical world (such as global warming) and tendencies in
the world of ideas (such as changes in what we find acceptable and unacceptable). Such a distinction will be clear enough in use, even if ultimately ideas
themselves have a physical basis.

Third, ideas do not have to be in people's heads to exist. Written media
record and convey ideas. If it makes any sense at all to quantify ideas, we can
surely say that the ideas that are 'out there' in libraries and on the internet far
outweigh what could be retained in a single person's head, and probably in
the heads of all people now living. (A classic statement of this point is in
Popper 1972).

If ideas exist in writing, then there is no reason to dispute that they can also exist in other media, such as painting and film, not to mention 'conceptual art'. And it is then only a slight extension to say that they exist in more or less standardised or ritualised patterns of behaviour. It seems quite intelligible, for instance, to say that the centuries-old rituals of the UK Parliament embody certain ideas about the relationship between constitutional monarchy and parliamentary democracy.

This section has attempted to unpack the idea of the ethical environment, as Blackburn uses that idea. As a complement to this approach, we can look at other ways and contexts in which we use the notion of environment.

The ethical environment compared with other environments

If we speak simply of 'the environment' we usually mean either the natural environment, or what Blackburn calls the physical environment. The physical environment is broader than the natural environment, since it includes the humanly altered and humanly constructed environment. The physical environment, both natural and humanly constructed, influences the kind of life we lead. Saharan Africa is a different environment from Arctic Scandinavia, and central London is still, despite globalisation, a different environment from downtown Tokyo, and people live and behave differently in these different environments.

If one assumes that 'the environment', properly so called, is the physical environment, then speaking of any other sort of environment will seem merely metaphorical. But there is no good reason to confine what we think of as our environment to physical features of the world only. We have other perfectly valid ways of using the term 'environment', such as *social environment*, and there is no reason to think that these ways are only metaphorical. At its most general, the term *environment* denotes something like the surroundings in which life goes on, and for human beings at least (and probably for many other species) these surroundings are never confined to physical features of the world.

Within intellectual enquiry into education, we can use the term 'environment' as a shorthand way of summing up all the influences on a person's life that are not genetically given. Some researchers argue over the proportional effects on adult IQ score of inheritance and upbringing; in other words, how much of the variation in IQ scores within a population is attributable to genetics, how much to environment. In such cases, 'environment' can cover a multitude of factors, which perhaps have in common only that they are not factors fixed genetically at birth. The term 'social environment' is just slightly less open-ended. It refers us to certain aspects of people's environment, to do with interpersonal relationships, the use of language, the conventions of society and so on.

Where does the *ethical environment* fit in? First, it is worth clearing away a possible misunderstanding about the term. The *term* 'ethical environment' is like the *term* 'social environment' in that the adjective is used to pick out a category of interest, not to make an evaluation. To speak of the *social* environment is to focus on certain aspects of human surroundings; it is not to pick out a certain environment as being good (because tending towards sociability) as opposed to being bad, or *anti*-social. We could if we wish say that some kind of environment is *anti-social*, but this would be to make a negative evaluation within the descriptive category of social environments. In a similar way, the term '*ethical* environment' is not meant to contrast with *unethical*, but to pick out the kind of features in which we are interested. If we were to call some kind of environment an *unethical* one, then we would be making a negative evaluation within the descriptive category of ethical environment. (There is a similar ambiguity between description and evaluation in the term *moral*. To describe an opinion as a moral opinion is usually to categorise the kind of opinion it is – roughly, that it is to do with matters of morality rather than, say, of aesthetics or of pure practicality. If, within the category of moral opinions, we are inclined to put a negative evaluation on someone's view, then we can use the term *immoral*, corresponding to *anti-social* or *unethical* in the other cases.)

Though the term 'social environment' gets its meaning partly by contrast with terms such as 'natural' or 'physical' environment, it does not follow that there is no overlap between the categories. We have no difficulty in recognising that the social environment of a child born to an impoverished family in a shanty town outside one of the world's largest cities is a different social environment from that of a child born to wealthy parents in the affluent suburbs of the same city. Part of the difference between these social environments consists in differences in factors such as family relationships and expectations, and possibly also in different ways of using language (different accents or different dialects); indeed we might want to speak separately of different linguistic environments. But the physical differences between the two environments, in housing, infrastructure, proximity of buildings, presence or absence of green spaces, are in themselves important factors in making one a different social environment from the other.

The same is true for terms such as 'school environment' or 'classroom environment'. These *may* be taken to refer primarily to physical features, but physical features that have been constructed or brought about by individual people: grass, or litter, in outdoor play areas; children's paintings, or graffiti, on walls. 'School environment' or 'classroom environment' may also be understood as referring to aspects of social interaction and expectations, that is, as variations on the terms 'ethos', 'school climate' and 'school culture' that have become well established in educational discourse (Prosser 1999; Glover and Coleman 2005; McLaughlin 2005). Either way, as the examples of litter, graffiti or paintings show, the physical and social environments cannot be sharply differentiated.

If the ethical environment overlaps with other kinds of environment that we may be more used to talking about, it might be asked whether we need the distinct term 'ethical environment'. The correct answer, as with many developments in terminology, is probably that we could manage without it, but that nevertheless it helps us to focus our attention on something well worth thinking about. While many of the arguments in this book might be expressed without using the term 'ethical environment', that could only be done by resorting to more familiar terminology, which would include such established terms as 'social environment', 'culture' and 'ethos'. But the very fact that such terms are so familiar means that the understanding of an argument may be distorted by what is already taken for granted. It may take a different vocabulary to shake us out of the connotations of a more familiar terminology. Besides, the familiar notions, being in common use, have a very broad range of meaning, whereas the terminology of 'the ethical environment', while still broad enough, gives us a more specific focus than simply 'social environment' or 'culture'.

The point that connotations can be misleading is well illustrated by 'culture'. We are used to an association between values and culture; indeed the idea that there are different cultures distinguished in part by their different values is so familiar that it needs in itself to be recognised as part of our contemporary ethical environment. More will be said about this idea in the next chapter. But we can already notice that the plural form, 'cultures', conveys connotations of distinctness. In the face of those connotations, any attempt to establish the view that there is a sense in which we all, worldwide, inhabit the same culture would be immediately implausible. In contrast, the term 'environment' helps us recognise that for the ethical environment as well as for the physical environment it makes sense to say that we all inhabit the same environment, even while we recognise differences that lead us to speak of different environments (there will be more later in this chapter on why both ways of speaking – sometimes of *the* ethical environment and sometimes of particular ethical environments – make sense).

We live in a world that we divide up conceptually for various purposes. We talk about the natural environment when we have certain aspects of our surroundings in mind, about the social environment when we have certain other aspects in mind, and so on for linguistic environment, built environment, academic environment, political environment – the list could be extended indefinitely. There will certainly be many overlaps in the phenomena that these terms refer to, but (if we keep that fact in mind) working with one particular category of environment can be an aid to focusing our thought.

At the same time, the overlapping nature of these conceptions will make it difficult to give a clear delineation of the ethical environment. Of course, it must have something to do with what we understand the scope of 'the ethical' to be, but that is itself a larger issue than can be settled by stipulating a definition. It may be better to start by recognising something of the great variety of ways in which environmental factors can make a difference to how people live and how they think.

Ethical influence of the physical environment

People respond to changes in the physical environment (both natural and humanly constructed or altered) in ways that would be widely recognised as moral or ethical, even in advance of further discussion of what these terms mean. Recent concern about global warming is a clear example. So are many more local concerns about the environmental impact of human developments. We have now a category, 'environmental ethics', which would hardly have been recognised a century ago, at least in the West. And we also may respond to events in the natural environment – such as the tsunami in the Indian Ocean in late December 2004, and Hurricane Katrina in the Gulf of Mexico and the earthquake in Pakistan and neighbouring areas in 2005 – in ways that draw on ethical concerns, not for the environment itself, but for other human beings.

It is not only that ethical thinking can respond to events in the physical environment. The physical environment in which people are located can itself make a difference to their ethical thinking, by making a difference to the kind of life that human beings find worth leading or possible to lead. This is worth remembering when questions are raised (as they will be raised later in this book) about the possible universality of certain values. It was possible for a vegetarian way of life, supported by a consistent set of values, to arise in the Indian sub-continent many centuries ago, when the same would not have been possible for humans north of the Arctic Circle.

A rather different way in which the physical environment can affect people's thinking is illustrated by events on Mount Everest in May 1996. Several teams of climbers were on the mountain at the same time, all facing severe difficulties in exceptionally poor weather. One team on their way to the summit passed two other climbers who were close to death. They did not stop to help. The two climbers passed were among nine who died on Everest that day. Interviewed later, one of the climbers who went past without stopping said 'Above 8,000 metres is not a place where people can afford morality' (Krakauer 1997: 241).

That is an example of an individual's thinking being affected by his immediate physical environment at a specific time. There is no point in speculating on what sort of morality would have developed within a society living above 8,000 metres, since no human society ever could have developed there in the absence of advanced technology. Whatever ideas of morality individuals operate with above that level, they have, so to speak, imported them from more normal conditions. And different individuals may make something different out of what they bring to the situation; not all mountaineers agree with the one quoted. (The term 'situation' rather than 'environment' in the last sentence anticipates a distinction to be made below.)

There are examples of a change in a community's natural environment affecting the morality of the whole community. The anthropologist Colin Turnbull (1974) reported on *The Mountain People*, the Ik. They were not originally mountain people, but a nomadic group of hunters ranging over a wide territory on the borders of Sudan, Uganda and Kenya. In the late 1930s they were encouraged to settle in a small mountainous region in Northern Uganda; the creation of a National Park in what had been their major hunting ground further confined them to the mountains and enforced a change in their way of life. There was little hunting left to them; they tried to grow their food, but the soil was poor. By the time Turnbull lived with them in the 1960s their social structure had thoroughly broken down. Rather than constituting a community the Ik (having dwindled to a population of about 2,000) seemed, on Turnbull's account, to be a collection of human beings among whom individualism and selfishness had been taken to extremes; cooperation and fellow feeling seemed virtually to have disappeared.

In much less extreme conditions, people's physical environment can make a difference to what kind of behaviour they find acceptable or unacceptable, what they are prepared to do or not to do. It seems to be a commonplace in architecture and urban planning that the nature of the housing in which people live (presence or absence of communal facilities, presence or absence of gardens, and so on) makes a difference to how people relate to their neighbours and to how far they take care of their surroundings. There can be positive feedback effects (an environment that is already pleasant makes it more likely that people will look after that environment), and negative feedback effects (if the place is already full of graffiti and litter, why bother?). Some public authorities take such effects into account in their policies on anti-social behaviour and law breaking; New York's 'broken windows' strategy is a case in point (Prime Minister's Strategy Unit 2004: 52; Gladwell 2001). When head teachers want their schools to be neat and tidy, it is not just for aesthetic reasons.

It appears that people do not have to be in a particular environment for a long time for it to make a difference to their behaviour. A group of researchers led by Robert Levine studied the extent to which people were willing to help strangers in different cities across the world. Rio de Janeiro and San José in Costa Rica turned out to be the cities in which strangers were most likely to be helped; helpfulness was least likely in Kuala Lumpur, New York, Singapore and Amsterdam. In any such study there will be a number of variables at play. The culture of the surrounding society – Latin American, European, East Asian – was one factor, but the differences could not be explained fully in this way. Another was the pace of life in the cities: for the most part, people were less helpful in cities with a fast pace of life. But the strongest indicator of differences appeared to be population density; people were less likely to help in cities with greater crowding (even when they were not in their own city). In the words of one commentator (*New Scientist*, 21 June 2003, p. 51) this suggests 'environment has a greater influence than ethnicity or cultural background'.

Refining 'the ethical environment'

The last section contained examples in which the physical environment made a difference to how people behave towards others. Should we count all of these examples as being cases of 'the ethical environment' in action? We *could* decide to do that. Certainly it is important, in the context of education, to recognise the potential influence of the physical environment on behaviour. And certainly an ethical environment and a physical environment may be closely interrelated. In the case of the Ik, if we were asked to describe the ethical environment in which they lived we would have to mention their apparent lack of concern for others, their tendency to laugh at others' misfortunes, their willingness to snatch whatever food they could for themselves; but it would be misleading to mention all of this without also referring to the imposed harshness of their physical environment.

Nevertheless, it will probably make for clarity if we concentrate on *ideas* when talking about the ethical environment. Blackburn speaks of 'the surrounding climate of ideas about how to live'. In some cases, as with the Ik, we can see how this climate has been influenced by the physical environment, but there are other cases in which a particular ethical environment appears largely independent of the physical. Take Blackburn's own first example: the Nazis.

The thought and the actions of the Nazis in Germany in the 1930s, leading into the Second World War and to the Holocaust in particular, have become part of common knowledge (though how far they continue to be so must at least in part be a question of education). Hitler as a personification of evil, and Nazism as an evil doctrine, have become part of the stock-in-trade of those who discuss ethical matters. In other words, an awareness of the horrors of Nazism has become part of our contemporary ethical environment. But for the moment our focus is not on our current ethical environment, but on that of 1930s Germany. It is widely recognised that what happened there cannot be wholly explained by the influence of one person or even of one doctrine. We can hardly avoid asking what it was about the climate of ideas at that time that made it possible for that person and that doctrine to gain so much ascendancy.

Blackburn lists several elements of that climate, including images of racial purity, fear of perceived threats to this purity, visions of national destiny, and more. These had their roots in 'misapplications of Darwinism, in German Romanticism, and indeed in some aspects of Judaism and Christianity' (Blackburn 2001: 3). These images, fears and hopes coloured the way that many Germans of the time were thinking. So it was not that Hitler was able to come to power because people ceased to think. Rather, 'Hitler could come to power only because people *did* think – but their thinking was poisoned by an enveloping climate of ideas, many of which may not even have been conscious' (Blackburn 2001: 3).

This climate of ideas, on the face of it, had nothing to do with a particular physical environment. The physical environment of twentieth-century Germany was not strikingly discontinuous with that of the rest of Europe, and there was nothing exceptionally harsh about it. The political and economic environment of Germany in the years after the First World War was far more directly implicated in the rise of Nazism. Yet even in this case the physical environment may have had some influence. Glover (1999), who devotes several chapters to analysing, in effect, the ethical environment in which Nazism flourished, mentions the importance in Nazi ideology of a sense of place: the primordial purity of the people to which Blackburn refers was seen as rooted in the German woods and forests. But it was not, of course, the day-to-day experience of living in the woods and forests that had the effect; most Germans in the 1930s did not live among the trees. It was the *idea* of the woods and forests that was a part (among many other constituents) of the ethical environment in which Nazism took hold.

In this book, the focus will be on *ideas*, but we should remember throughout that ideas do not exist only in the heads of individuals. Ideas, including that range of ideas about what is desirable or undesirable, good or bad, that we call *values*, can be embodied in human institutions and practices of many kinds. It is at least arguable (though the argument of this book does not depend on this) that values have no existence independently of the human practices in which they are embodied (Raz 2003). But even if values do in some way exist independently of human practices and discourse, it is still, at least very largely, through practices, institutions and discourse that people come to be aware of values and to be influenced by them: a point that *is* central to this book. Education, of course, forms a vital part of these practices, institutions and discourse.

Just what range of ideas should we see as constituting the *ethical* environment? They will be ideas that influence people's views about what is acceptable and unacceptable behaviour, about what they owe to others, about which ways of living are best, and so on. No apology is needed here for the indication of vagueness in 'and so on'; we cannot put clear demarcations around the range of ideas that constitute the ethical environment. The most obvious candidates are ideas that are directly *about* conduct and about the evaluation of persons or of ways of living: so notions such as 'right' and 'wrong', 'good' and 'bad' will count as part of the ethical environment, and the particular interpretation put on such terms may be part of what constitutes a particular ethical environment. In contrast, it may seem obvious that there are some ideas that have nothing to do with ethics: ideas, for instance, in the sciences. But while there may well be ways in which science can be and should be 'value-free', that does not mean that scientific ideas cannot influence people's thinking about how to live and about what is acceptable. We have already seen one example, in Blackburn's mention of a misapplication of Darwinism as part of the Nazi climate of ideas. Even ideas about the origins of the universe, apparently far removed from any questions about human conduct, *can* influence people's ethical thinking. The connection might go something like this: cosmology seems to be able to explain the origins of the universe without bringing in God; therefore there is no God; therefore the universe is an entirely physical state of matter and energy devoid of values; therefore there are no values apart from what humans think up for themselves; therefore there is nothing objective or binding about any of our values.

While there are several large gaps in that argument as it stands, it may still be recognisable as part of a certain kind of secular outlook. Whether it is a good argument or not, it can be part of our ethical environment, since that environment can contain bad arguments and false claims as well as good arguments and true claims. The present point is that it may be difficult to think of any ideas of which the content is so unconnected with human life that they cannot have a bearing on ethical thinking. It is impossible, then, to put any sharp limits around the range of ideas that might be counted as part of the ethical environment.

Does this mean that the notion of the ethical environment is too open-ended to be of any use? Does it have no more (but no less) usefulness than talk of the spirit of the times (*zeitgeist*) or the current cultural climate? We can give a rather more specific sense to the idea of the ethical environment. The way that we talk about the physical environment may help to illustrate the point. We know well enough for practical purposes what we mean when we express concerns about 'the environment': global warming, damage to the ozone layer, destruction of rain forests, and so on. But what counts as part of the physical environment? Given that it has to include, not just the natural environment, but also items that have been produced or altered by human beings (cities, transport systems, rubbish, waste heat, etc.) it may be hard to think of anything that is a material object or that involves a physical process that could *not* be counted as part of 'the environment'. Nevertheless, at least within a certain context of discussion and given certain purposes, we can have a workable sense of what to treat as the salient aspects of the environment. The indeterminacy of the notion does not prevent us working with it.

Similarly, while almost any idea, any way of thinking, could be a part of the ethical environment, that does not stop us discerning certain aspects of our human world that are particularly salient, perhaps at a certain time or in a certain place, to our thinking about 'how to live'. This book, in using the idea of the ethical environment rather than something like the cultural climate or *zeitgeist*, will be giving particular attention to those elements of our social and linguistic environment that have in fact drawn the attention of that branch of philosophy called 'moral philosophy' or 'ethics'. These include ideas of right and wrong, obligation, virtue, the good life and well-being, which will be explored further in the first part of the next chapter.

Some questions of terminology

An initial indication has been given of the concerns that will be included under 'the ethical environment' within this book. If that terminology is to be recommended for more general use, then some further terminological issues may arise that can usefully be anticipated here.

'Moral' and 'ethical'

Blackburn's initial gloss on the idea referred to 'the moral or ethical environment'. Many people would find no awkwardness in using 'moral' and 'ethical' interchangeably. Others would argue that it makes for clarity in our thinking to recognise that what we call 'morality' does not exhaust our ethical concerns and interests. In other words, morality may be only a part of the ethical environment – a view that will be explained further in the next chapter. Since there is the possibility that 'moral environment' might convey something different from 'ethical environment', only the second term will be used here.

'Environment' and 'situation'

The majority of the human actions that we evaluate, whether as right or wrong, good or bad, generous or mean, or whatever, are responses to some situation. Perhaps another person is in some perceived need; the occasion for redeeming a promise comes up; there is a request for information, raising the possibility of telling the truth or not; a person is in financial difficulties, and wonders whether to borrow money with no intention of paying it back (Kant 1785: 67, 85).

Consider one of the most notorious (and arguably one of the most illuminating) series of experiments in social psychology: Stanley Milgram's electric shock experiments.[2] Individuals in the United States were asked by the experimenter, ostensibly as part of an experiment on learning, to administer electric shocks of increasing intensity to the learners when they failed to learn. In actuality the learners were actors who did not suffer any real shocks; the real subjects of the experiment were the people asked to deliver the shocks. The experiments were conducted in a number of forms with changes in several variables (Milgram 1974). The central finding throughout was that many people would administer what they believed to be real and powerful electric shocks to others, on the instructions of the experimenter.

The *situation* here was the experimental set-up, in which an individual had agreed to take part in an experiment run by a respectable scientist (often a person in a white coat in a university laboratory) for the sake of advancing knowledge about how people learn. The surrounding ethical *environment* was one in which there was a certain widespread respect for and deference to academics, for scientists, perhaps for anyone who appeared to be legitimately in authority. Many people felt they had to obey, that it would be wrong not to go along with the experimenter's request, even that they would be letting the experimenter down or subverting the experiment itself if they refused to press the switches that (they believed) were delivering intense shocks to the 'learners'.

Of course, what those individuals did was in part a function of the situation in which they found themselves, and in part, arguably, a function of certain individual tendencies which may have been differentially present in those who did and in those who did not obey. But we need the third factor too to make sense of what was going on: the broader ethical environment of the experimenter and all the subjects.

It is unlikely always to be clear just where the line can be drawn between the immediate situation and the broader ethical environment, but to be able to mark the distinction will help us ask interesting questions about the relationship between individual action, individual character (see Chapter 3) and the wider climate of ideas.

'Environment' and 'climate'

To this point the present discussion has followed Blackburn in drawing no explicit distinction between 'environment' and 'climate'. In the context of the physical environment we would surely have to say that climate constitutes only one part, or only one set of aspects, of the environment. Not all concern about the environment is a concern about climate.

In the ethical context, whether it is worth making a distinction between 'environment' and 'climate' is a question of whether there is any useful distinction that we can mark by differentiating the terms. It is possible to think of the ethical environment as encompassing the whole range of ideas that can impinge on our ethical thinking and that are available to us: the ideas that are, so to speak, 'out there' in the environment, whether or not they are especially salient to particular individuals or particular communities. But a climate of ideas, as Blackburn uses the term, is clearly not just a *set* of ideas; it is a particular conjunction of ideas, giving salience to some ideas rather than to others, making particular connections between some ideas and others. We might try, then, to use the term 'ethical environment' in the broad sense, to encompass all the ideas available to us that are relevant to our thinking about how to live, and the term 'ethical climate' to refer to some discernable tendency or pattern of ideas in a particular part of the world, or salient to a particular human concern (within *the* environment, one would notice the climate changing, or notice different climates in different areas). But the difficulty of following such a usage consistently, with the consequent demarcation problems it would bring, would probably outweigh any benefits to be gained. As already mentioned, it is an advantage of the term 'environment' that it allows us quite consistently to speak of many environments and of one environment.

Many environments and one environment

In the physical case, we can, of course, recognise different environments, such as those of Saharan Africa, the lands around the Arctic Circle, central South

America, Himalayan Asia. But we have also become used to talking about '*the* environment'. Sometimes this is merely a shorthand way of referring to whichever surrounding environment is particularly salient to us at the time. But we can also, as it were, speak of The Environment, a singular entity. This is global. We know now that what happens in one part of the world (emissions from factories and vehicles, for instance) can have an effect on what happens in some far removed part (such as the Antarctic ice shelf). There are no sharp discontinuities between one bit of The Environment and another.

We can follow the same pattern in using the notion of 'ethical environment'. We can distinguish different ethical environments. The ethical environment of Germany at the beginning of the twenty-first century, for instance, is very different from what it was in the late 1930s. The distinctions we make between cultures are in part distinctions between ethical environments, as we shall see in the next chapter. As in the physical case, when it is obvious which particular environment we have in mind, we can refer to it simply as 'the environment'.

Does it also, however, make sense to speak, as it were, of *The* Ethical Environment? Perhaps it would not have made sense until quite recently, but it does now. That it makes sense now is one element of globalisation. Of course, to suggest that there is one global ethical environment is not to deny all the differences that exist, any more than speaking of the physical environment is to deny differences between one place and another. But it is to suggest that, ethically as well as physically, no part of the world is hermetically sealed off from all others.

The interaction of education and the ethical environment

If there is one overarching argument of this book, it is that our thinking about education should take more account of the ethical environment, and of the connections between that environment and education, than it usually does now. Those connections work interactively in two directions. Education is important to the quality of the ethical environment; and the ethical environment has an important bearing on the nature and quality of education at a particular time and place.

Regarding the first direction – the difference education makes to the quality of the ethical environment – the precise description of the relationship depends not only on how broadly we take 'the ethical environment', but also on how broadly we understand 'education'. If we take 'education' in its broadest possible sense, to cover all knowledge, capacities, attitudes and achievements that come about through learning – very roughly, everything that is owed to 'nurture', not 'nature' – then it would be possible to argue that almost everything in the ethical environment is there as a result of education. This is not to deny that there may well be capacities and dispositions in human beings, relevant to the ethical environment, that are biologically inherited: an example would be the capacity for and tendency towards altruism, which many evolutionary psychologists have argued could, despite appearances, be an outcome of natural selection. But such capacities, even if present in all individuals at birth, need to be developed within a social setting, and may remain relatively undeveloped if the social setting does not support their development through example and expectation. In the environment of the Ik, for instance, there was little that would nurture the capacities of empathy and altruism. In more sophisticated societies, there may be deliberate attempts to mould the ethical environment through the content and ethos of schooling and other institutions; we often use the term 'indoctrination' for such attempts. But it does not follow, from the fact that we make a distinction between 'indoctrination' and 'education', that there is any kind of education that will not make a difference to the ethical environment. How far societies may justifiably use educational measures to influence the ethical environment will be one of the concerns of this book, especially in Chapter 5.

If education inescapably influences the ethical environment, then equally the ethical environment, as part of the context in which education goes on, influences the nature of that education. This again is true however widely we interpret 'education', but it will be appropriate now to give some examples where the influence is on schooling.

The point intended here is not the familiar one that the ethos of the school itself is important to the nature and quality of the learning that goes on within it (McLaughlin 2005). Indeed, important as school ethos is, it is not impossible for thinking about the quality of schooling to focus *too exclusively* on the ethos of individual schools. Too exclusive a focus would be one that missed the importance of the surrounding ethical environment that is shared by all schools, or all schools of a given kind. Government policy in England, for instance, at the time of writing, seeks to encourage different schools to develop and proclaim their distinctive ethos. And there are indeed many ways in which schools, even within the category of comprehensive schools within a state system, may differ from each other in their ethos. But at the same time the ethos of all will be influenced by their being all situated within one broader ethical environment – an environment that is itself in part formed by government policy, as we shall see below.

We have already seen that we can speak both of particular ethical environments – characterising, say, life in particular countries at particular times – and of a global ethical environment. Within education, it is possible to study the effects on schooling of the ethical environment of a particular country. An example is the research of Mirembe and Davies (2001) on school ethos in Uganda. Their report in this article focuses on one particular school, in which the ethos is strikingly sexist; in the words of their abstract, the school is characterised by 'hegemonic masculinity, gendered discipline patterns, sexual harassment and "compulsory" heterosexuality' (Mirembe and Davies 2001: 401). But their research also suggests that this ethos is in many ways continuous with the wider ethos of much of Ugandan life.

Many societies may now pride themselves on having moved away in recent years from the worst manifestations of sexism and homophobia. But there may be other features of the ethical environment in, say, Britain or the United States that can call forth damning criticism from commentators. In November 2005 the Children's Commissioner for England, in his first report in his new post, said 'I have no doubt that children are being brought up in a society where violence is the norm. I include in this the violence on television, in the workplace and in the home. Violence is part of our contemporary culture, where it is so prevalent that it largely goes unremarked' (Hill 2005). The commissioner was explicitly linking that wider culture with the problem of bullying in schools. This recognition of the influence of the wider ethical environment on the ethos within schools is surely correct, even if the perception that 'violence is the norm' is arguably an exaggeration.

Brighouse (2006), following Schor 2004, focuses on a different feature of contemporary society: commercialism. His heaviest criticism in this respect is of the United States, while he considers that in the United Kingdom 'commercialism is less pervasive, but still incredibly powerful' (Brighouse 2006: 49). In his view 'the cultural environment most of us inhabit now is one in which the most powerful forces attempting to shape the culture are driven by the desire to make large profits' (p. 50). Since these forces can easily come to permeate schools, he would prefer to see 'a school with an ethos that is not exactly countercultural, but perhaps extra-popular-cultural' (p. 60).

It is a further question how far it is possible for a school to achieve and maintain an ethos that is independent of the nature of the surrounding ethical environment. In the case of commercialism, there is a tendency in the governance of schools in many countries that arguably is another face of commercialism: the tendency summed-up in the term 'marketisation'. Where the wider culture of commercialism encourages the view that everything that is worthwhile in life is available for buying and selling, there is some evidence that the introduction of the market into the organisation of the schooling system itself may undermine moral integrity.

What are the effects on those who work in schools of an environment in which schools are expected to compete with each other, in which, as in businesses, there are targets to be met, and in which the penalties for failing to meet those targets may, as in business, be financial ones? Ball (2003) cites a number of cases in English schools in which heads and senior managers in schools have 'fiddled' or 'massaged' their figures. Referring to a Deputy Head in a London school who is quoted by Davies (2000) as saying: 'I don't feel any shame about it at all. There is no other way to do it. And that's the truth. Everybody does it', Ball remarks: 'The Deputy Head's comments are particularly telling. Indicative perhaps of the changes taking place here. He feels no shame – the implication is that the ethical environment is not such that these actions attract criticism or stigma – in part at least because "everybody does it" ' (Ball 2003: 209).[3]

Another commentator on the nature of school management in modern times, Bottery, has a similar account of the effects of market forms of accountability. He reports: 'There is evidence that, under current target-driven regimes, some individuals do manage to work the system successfully, as they knowingly 'play the game' while at the same time keeping their eye on "the real" issues, needs and desired developments of their organizations' (Bottery 2004: 90).

The Deputy Head quoted by Ball *may* be among those individuals who can work the system with integrity, putting priority on his pursuit of educational values while consciously adapting to the demands of an ethical environment with which he does not really identify. On the other hand, he may have lost his 'moral compass'.[4] Bottery goes on to report, citing Jeffrey and Woods (1998) and Hargreaves (2003), that many teachers (not only those in leadership roles) find that knowingly 'playing the game' makes them lose their self-respect and feel demoralised.

When we think seriously about the relationship between schooling and the ethical environment, one question has to be whether the surrounding ethical climate supports schools, including all those who work in them, in doing what schools ought to be doing. But what is it that schools ought to be doing? I want to argue that we cannot give a full answer to that question without taking the ethical environment into account, in all its rich diversity. It is to that diversity of the ethical environment that I turn in the next chapter.

2 The diversity of the ethical environment

'Diversity' means 'variety', 'heterogeneity'. In recent years in some circles 'diversity' has come to have a more specialised meaning, referring to heterogeneity among persons in certain specified dimensions: ethnicity and culture, gender, sexual orientation. But to concentrate on these dimensions is to neglect the sheer variety of the constituents of our – anyone's – ethical environment.

In this chapter I want above all to bring out this internal diversity in the ethical environment. I shall deliberately not try to do this culture by culture. All the kinds of ideas I mention are likely to be found in many, if not all, human cultures. I shall not try to demonstrate that here. This is one of the points where philosophy is, in effect, saying 'Look and see. It is like this, isn't it?' It is calling attention to something that, because it is part of everyday experience, can easily be overlooked in an academic context. Every reader, from whatever cultural background he or she comes, should see if these ideas are familiar. Only later in the chapter shall I say something explicitly about cultural difference.

In general, it must be education – taking the term in its broadest sense – that perpetuates the ideas and ways of thinking that make up the diversity of the ethical environment. Within that generalisation, there are many questions that can be asked about the specific role of formal education, or schooling. While some of these questions will be raised in this chapter, it will be the next chapter that will begin to look more systematically at how the diversity of the ethical environment can be reflected and accommodated within education.

Ethical animals

A good starting point here will be some minimally controversial truisms about human beings. These are observations about what human beings are like, not about how human beings came to be like this or why. So they should be compatible, for instance, both with naturalistic accounts that hold that it simply happened that human beings evolved as they did, and with theological accounts that hold that there is a divine design behind human nature. Of course, the fact that both theological and naturalistic accounts can be given about human nature (and that many people think these are compatible, but some do not) is itself an important feature of our ethical environment. But that is a point for later.

Human beings are social animals. For many of the satisfactions of life they need to be with others, cooperating with others, often dependent on others. They are communicating, language-using animals. They have since ancient times been called rational animals. That means, not that they always think or act rationally rather than irrationally, but that they have the capacity to think about what they are doing, to make decisions rather than behaving instinctively. And they can consciously follow rules, and consciously break them. They are also feeling animals. Human beings *care* about what happens; they can experience things as mattering to them (they can even care about being rational). They have a sense of the future, and can aim at goals. And they are vulnerable. They can be damaged and can suffer physically and be hurt emotionally.

Human beings are also, as Blackburn (2001: 4) comments, ethical animals. In fact if all the other points just made are true, it is probably inevitable that they will be ethical animals. That is to say, they evaluate: they like some things and dislike other things; they are sometimes pleased and sometimes disappointed; they think some things are worth aiming at and other things better avoided; they think their lives are sometimes going well and sometimes going badly. At every turn they are responding positively or negatively to something. All these evaluations happen in the context of communication; we can communicate our evaluations to others, including our evaluations of them and their actions, and we are influenced by their evaluations. (Perhaps this is not true of some basic likings or preferences, but reflection on the prevalence of fashion, not confined to clothes or music, shows that even what we like is far from being free of influence.) If there were rational but atomistic animals that could evaluate things but were not social and had no communication, they would not live in an ethical environment; but we humans do.

Constituents of the ethical environment

We can already begin to see something of the range of evaluations we make. Even if we begin with wants and preferences, we can easily see that our wants do not concern just ourselves. Being social animals, we have many wants that refer to others. We can want good relations with others, we can want cooperation with others, and it is also possible to want to have power over others. We can want our family or our country, or even the human race, to be doing well. We *can*, but may not always.

Social animals, with such capacities for evaluation, and capable of following rules, are bound to develop a sense of norms about how they should treat each other. (The point of the locution 'develop *a sense of* norms' is that the thought that such norms are not simply human creations is not being ruled out; if the norms have some other kind of origin or basis, it is still true that human beings have to recognise them.) Such norms include prohibitions or limits on causing injury to others, and may also include expectations of help for others in need. They may include expectations of cooperation in joint enterprises, and also expectations of non-interference in what individuals do by themselves. They may include the recognition of possessions for the use of individuals or their families, of which others are not to deprive them. They will certainly include some norms regulating communication, such as a general expectation that truth is to be told, perhaps with recognised exceptions, and recognition of some statements of intent for the future as constituting promises, which are to be kept. All human societies have developed norms about how individuals are to conduct themselves as they relate to others, though sometimes the application of those norms may not have been extended outside the immediate group. It hardly needs to be said that within any group it is a function of education – at least in the broadest informal sense – to see that these norms do not die out in each generation.

To some people, norms such as those just mentioned represent what *morality* essentially is about: what we owe to each other, expressed in rules that say 'do this' and 'don't do that'. Such a view of morality often incorporates some underlying assumptions: that human beings are so constituted that their lives as social beings will not necessarily be harmonious; that they have individual interests that can conflict with those of other individuals; that they tend to give special weight to their self-interest; that given these facts and their vulnerabilities, they need a degree of protection against each other.

This picture makes morality in some ways quite similar to the law of states, the law that is made by legislators and obeyed or broken by subjects or citizens. Like the law of states, it has to be taken seriously if it is to do something to mitigate human vulnerabilities. The law of states is backed up by the possibility of coercive sanctions, but many people will abide by the law because they have come to have a degree of respect for it. The rules of morality – if it is understood in this way – also have to be seen as, like laws, being in some way binding. These rules have not been decided on and issued by a human legislator. Perhaps they have been issued by a divine legislator (nothing in the present argument precludes that) and are backed up by sanctions of a different kind. Perhaps they have no legislator but can still be experienced as having some kind of special force and demandingness. If the rules are recognised and taken sufficiently seriously they can have their effect within human societies, whatever their source.

Some such conception of morality is a widespread aspect of the ethical environment in which many human beings live. But it probably does not capture the whole of most people's understanding of morality. What has sometimes been called '*morality in the narrow sense*' is a socially recognised set of constraints on conduct, where those constraints are taken sufficiently seriously to have some effect in protecting people in their vulnerability to each other.[1] The importance of morality in this narrow sense, and also the extent to which it has similarities with law, is indicated by the special vocabulary that has developed around it. In English, this vocabulary includes such notions as *duty, obligation, moral law,* (morally) *right,* (morally) *wrong,* and (quite recently in human history) *moral rights* or *human rights.*

It should be clear already that there must be more to the ethical environment than people's conception of morality in this narrow sense. When you reflect on other elements that are part of our ethical environment, you may want to include some, or even all, of these elements within your understanding of morality in some broader sense. On the other hand, you may find that some aspects of the ethical environment seem to you to be not part of morality at all. Some philosophers (including Williams 1985) have made a distinction between *morality* (in some fairly narrow sense concerning what we owe to each other) and *ethics*, which covers the whole field of evaluations concerned with how we are to live our lives. Though this is a useful distinction, it is not one that is consistently marked in common usage. There is little point in trying to stipulate any precise demarcations around *morality*; the important point here is that in exploring what is involved in the ethical environment, we have to go beyond the notion of morality in its narrow sense, as simply a set of norms constraining our conduct.

Why do we have to go beyond that? One reason is that norms specifying or prohibiting certain conduct say nothing directly about feelings and motives. This is another way in which morality in the narrow sense can be like the law of states, which to a large extent is concerned to regulate conduct, not to regulate feelings and motives. The law may take motivation into account when prescribing penalties for law-breaking, but for the most part its concern is with *what* people do or do not do. Provided people stay within the law, it does not matter (in the eyes of the law itself) whether they stay within the law through respect for the law, or through some moral sense that may be independent of the law; or through fear of punishment if they are caught breaking the law; or out of sheer habit, or whatever. What may be true of law, however, is not true of human life in general, and hence also not true of education. Education's concern with norms cannot be limited to trying to make sure that people follow the norms, regardless of their reasons.

Human beings are interested in feelings and motivation, and these come within the range of what we evaluate. If one person's conduct towards another never violates the other's rights, and is always within the bounds of civility and politeness, we can still think it makes a difference whether the first person respects the other, or is putting on an outward show of respect while actually despising the other. We may sometimes consider that motives make, not just some difference, but all the difference. Think of the debate over euthanasia where a person is terminally ill and in great and continuing distress (and take the question to be, not whether the law of states should allow euthanasia, but whether an act of euthanasia can ever be morally permissible). Some people will think in terms of a moral law that forbids killing, whatever the motive. Others will think that an act of euthanasia that is carried out in compassion, with the aim of sparing the victim from suffering and indignity, is permissible – perhaps even admirable.

Even if morality is framed in terms of laws about conduct, it would be a mistake to think that it can function independently of feeling. As noted above, the rules of morality even in the narrowest sense do not make a difference to human action simply by existing, but by being taken sufficiently seriously. That means that people have to *care* about whether the rules are followed. When others break the rules, we may feel anger or resentment towards them. When others know that we have broken the rules, we may feel ashamed; and even if no one else knows, we may feel guilt. The laws of the state impose sanctions on those who break them; morality has its own kind of sanctions in such feelings as guilt and resentment; and the desire to avoid guilt on one's own part, or the disapproval of others, is one kind of motivation for following the rules. We may have moral norms or conventions concerning what is felt, not just what is done. We may think that someone who has received a great benefit ought to *feel* gratitude, not just express it; we may think it is *right* that someone who has been maliciously injured feels resentment (Gibbard 1990).

So the first reason why we have to move beyond the idea of morality as a set of rules is that we need to take feelings and motivation into account. Another reason is that we know that rules, and the obligations to which they give rise, can conflict. Suppose you have promised a friend that you will not reveal some secret of theirs; but then you find yourself in a situation in which the only way to avoid revealing that secret would be by telling a lie. If you thought of this situation purely in terms of moral rules, of which one is 'don't break promises' and another is 'don't tell lies', then there would be no way of avoiding doing something wrong. That is a situation where a conflict can arise within interpersonal relationships; other cases of conflict arise because we have obligations and responsibilities that go with the various roles which we occupy. In modern societies, just as life is often divided up and may be to some degree compartmentalised into different roles, so there may be different responsibilities corresponding to different roles, and there can be no guarantee that the demands of different roles will be compatible. The work/life balance of which so much is now heard, in countries where full-time paid employment is normal, is not just a matter of individuals finding some balance that suits them personally; there can be real conflicts between obligations to employers and obligations to family.

What do we actually do in situations where rules or responsibilities conflict? We are likely to engage in some attempt at weighing up a variety of factors, going well beyond any rules that we think are involved. These might be, for instance, considerations about loyalty to a friend, about honesty, about trustworthiness. Such considerations do not themselves function as *rules*. We *can* formulate prescriptions such as 'be loyal', 'be honest', and so on, but prescriptions like these do not give the determinate kind of guidance that we may expect from rules. The notions involved now are much broader considerations that we may take into account. We could refer to these broader considerations as *principles* rather than rules. (This is yet another useful distinction, where rules tell you what to do or what not to do with little latitude for interpretation, whereas principles are considerations you should take into account but which leave much greater room for interpretation (Haydon 1999: 93; 107). But the distinction would be one of degree, and again it is not one that is consistently marked in ordinary English.) Or we may simply refer to these broader considerations such as 'loyalty' and 'honesty' as *values*.

Of course, when we decide what to do we are not always trying to follow moral rules or even broader principles. Sometimes we may be following our own preferences (which may already refer to others, and may have been formed as a result of our environment). Sometimes we may be acting out of care and concern for others, because the welfare of others (some others, at least) matters to us. Often it is the fact that we *do* care what happens to others that makes our decisions difficult.

One thing we can do in situations where there is no clear guidance to be had from thinking in terms of moral rules is to look at the consequences of one action or another. People sometimes think that morality must be more than a matter of trying to do what will have the best consequences; and they are probably quite right to think that. Sometimes recognising that you have an *obligation* to do something, or recognising that someone else has a *right* to something from you, means that you recognise that what you have to do is already settled regardless of consequences (that is part of the way that notions such as 'obligation' and 'rights' function). But where no such considerations settle the question in advance, often the only sensible thing to do is to look at the consequences of acting in one way rather than another. Of course, the consequences themselves have to be compared and evaluated. That brings us into another area of evaluation, where we have to evaluate a state of affairs. A decision between doing one thing and doing another, where either course of action will make a difference to others, is a decision between two states of affairs: the situation that we think will result from one course of action and the situation we think will result from another. Different people may be quite differently affected in the two situations. How do we compare the situations? Some philosophers have thought that it is always, at least in theory, possible to make the comparison in terms of happiness, so that we should do what will promote the greatest degree of happiness achievable (this would be a simple version of *utilitarianism*; most versions have been more complex). But if we try to go further into thinking what would count as 'making someone happy', we get straight into the complicated business of evaluating what is worth having in life.

For the last few paragraphs the focus has been on the kinds of factors people take into account in deciding what to do in particular situations (recall the distinction between 'situation' and 'environment' from the previous chapter). But we do not only evaluate *actions* – as right or wrong, a good thing to do or not, and so on. As just mentioned, we can evaluate states of affairs, and these may be much broader than the immediate consequences of a particular action. We can make some sort of evaluation of a whole life, or most of a life. It may be 'most of a life' when young people try to decide what they want to do with their lives. What would be a desirable kind of life to lead? What are the factors that come into that? But we do not only evaluate lives when we have decisions to make. A person can look back on her life, wondering whether it has on the whole been a good life, even when she thinks the answer to the question will make no difference because there is nothing she can do about it now.[2]

We can also ask whether other people's lives are good ones or not. In fact we can ask that question in more than one sense. We may be asking whether someone has led a *morally* good life (where 'morally good' might at its narrowest mean 'conforming to morality in the narrow sense', or might be interpreted somewhat more broadly). Or we may be asking about someone's quality of life: whether they are living, or have led, a life that seems good to them, brings them satisfaction, and so on. The two sorts of evaluation may be difficult to separate. You might think that Nelson Mandela, despite having spent so much of his life in prison, has led a good life, because you think that the deprivation of those years has been outweighed by what has come later – which may include both Mandela's own sense of satisfaction in what he has achieved, *and* the great value of those achievements, in your own estimation.

The question that philosophers often express as 'what is the good life?' has become important in recent philosophical discussion of education, since for many philosophers of education (e.g. White 1990, 2002; Brighouse 2006) a central aim of education is the good life, or the flourishing, of individuals. At the same time it may be impossible to say what a good life for an individual consists of without reference to the nature of the society in which the individual lives, given that human beings are social animals. Many of the evaluations we make are of societies or of social states of affairs. A society may be *just*, or *well ordered*, or *authoritarian*, or *anarchic*, and so on. Views of what is a good society may also feed into thinking about educational aims, since education may have social as well as individual aims (a point to which we shall return in the next chapter). If we start from the idea of human beings as social animals, we have to add that unlike other social animals they are *political* animals (a point that goes back to Aristotle). That is, they are capable, with their rational, communicative and cooperative capacities, of the deliberate organisation of their affairs. A large part of the human activities of evaluation, recommendation, criticism and so on is political in this sense.[3]

We evaluate actions, we evaluate states of affairs, and we also evaluate persons. It is not just that we can use the most general categories of evaluation – good and bad – about persons as well as about actions and states of affairs, but also that we have rich vocabularies for describing the qualities of persons in a way that is approving or disapproving. Examples in English are 'kind', 'generous', 'fair-minded', 'mean', 'self-centred', 'callous' and many more. For such qualities, when they are seen as desirable, there is an ancient term, which philosophers have been reviving in recent years. That term is 'virtues' (its opposite could be 'vices', though that has come to have a different sense in everyday English). Though the *word* 'virtues' may not currently be a salient part of the ethical environment for most of us, the various notions we have of particular desirable and admirable qualities certainly are. We can think about the desirable qualities that we might wish to have ourselves, and about the qualities we would hope to see in others (including our own children). Such qualities are often complex ones, involving perception, feeling, motivation and action. Suppose we hope that a child will turn out to be kind towards others: we shall want the child to *notice* when others are upset or liable to be hurt; to *care* about this; to *want* to help; and actually – at least on many occasions – to *do* something to help. Anything less may amount, not to having the virtue of kindness, but just to paying lip service to an idea of kindness.[4]

The kinds of idea mentioned so far may cover much of our thinking, not just about how we relate to each other (the sphere of 'morality in the narrow sense'), but about what is desirable and undesirable beyond that. It can cover, for instance, most debate about the treatment of animals. Concerns about the treatment of animals are an important aspect of at least some local ethical environments, but they do not necessarily bring in any new ethical notions. We can think about human treatment of sentient animals using utilitarian notions (if their suffering outweighs our pleasure in eating them, that is already a weighty argument for vegetarianism), and using notions about virtues (a tendency to be cruel to animals is bad), and some people, more controversially, ascribe rights to animals.

What has been mentioned so far, however, certainly does not exhaust the repertoire of ideas available within the ethical environment. For a reminder of one area that may be illuminating to the concerns of this book, we have only to go back to Blackburn's initial comparison. We have become sensitive, he said, to the physical environment; we know it is fragile, and we have the power to ruin it. The thought that we might ruin it is, of course, an evaluative notion. To ruin it would be to change it irrevocably for the worse. We cannot have this sensitivity to the physical environment without having a sense of what is better or worse for the environment. Perhaps there have always been some human societies that have had such a sense, but for many of us these ideas are becoming increasingly salient constituents of our own ethical environment. What sorts of ideas are these? Some of them involve simply extending our use of notions that are already familiar from our thinking about what humans owe to each other. If we think we should try to avoid courses of action that will have bad consequences for our descendents, that gives us good reason to avoid damaging the environment that our descendants will depend on. If we care about other people, not just those near to us in place and time but also those of future generations, then again we have reason to look after the environment. But it is also possible to have a regard for the natural environment that goes beyond its instrumental value to human beings and even to other animals. Some people might express this in terms of reverence or an attitude of piety towards the world; some, using the language of morality in a narrower sense, would consider that it is *wrong* to damage the environment, independently of any effects on sentient animals. Fewer people think that mountains and trees have *rights*. But there are other clusters of ideas that are relevant: aesthetic notions such as beauty, and notions that may be best classed as spiritual, such as 'awe' and 'wonder'. Besides, many of our descriptions of the natural environment – 'untouched', 'wilderness' and so on – have come to have evaluative connotations.

Though the catalogue has been far from exhaustive, the final set of ideas to be mentioned here – religious ideas – raises some new issues. With religion come some evaluative notions – including 'holy', 'saintly', 'sinful', 'blasphemous' – that would not exist in a world without religion, and some conceptions of what makes a good life that are not available independently of religious conceptions. In this exploration of the ethical environment it is not necessary to raise questions about the *truth* of religious beliefs. It is enough that beliefs about God (and some non-theistic beliefs about the nature of the universe that may be classed as religious) are important to millions of people and clearly overlap (to put the connection in the most minimal way) with thinking about what is right and good and desirable. In that sense religious ideas, while far more salient to some people than to others, are part of the ethical environment of all of us, and this book will have to revisit their place in this environment.

So far we have been looking at 'constituents' of an ethical environment, as so many different kinds of factors that can impinge on any person. Just what range of factors is actually salient to a particular individual will depend in part on the individual's immediate social environment, and in part on the role played by formal education. A person might be brought up in a family in which religious language is never used; or in a family in which no ethical concern about the physical environment is ever expressed; or perhaps in a family in which the notions of right and wrong are hardly used (for in certain environments, while terms that describe and evaluate persons and actions in terms of particular qualities – terms such as 'generous' and 'mean' – may be commonly used, there is a reluctance to label actions 'right' or 'wrong'). At the same time, it is unlikely in a modern society that individuals will not become aware, through their contact with others or through the media, that there is a wider range of ideas and concerns in the wider ethical environment than may appear in their immediate environment. One question about the role of formal education is how far it should be taking the responsibility to make everyone aware of the diversity and richness of the ethical environment; another question is how far it should be encouraging individuals actually to make use of a wide range of the linguistic resources available for ethical evaluation (Haydon 1999: 124–126).

Yet another question for education is how far it can help individuals in integrating – if integration is possible at all – the diverse elements of the ethical environment that they experience. We have already noted the 'work/ life balance' as one area of tension. There are others that may go still deeper: between materialistic and religious aspirations, for instance. Some ethical environments may contain more potential tensions than others; and some education systems may do more than others to help people to handle the tensions (while most societies, for instance, use schools to prepare people for paid employment, how many prepare people to handle the work/life balance?)

Interpretation and disagreement

We have been distinguishing different *kinds* of notion that are available to us within our ethical environment. Any of these kinds of notion is subject to differing interpretations (and education can, of course, influence the interpretations that people make). The most obvious differences but by no means the only ones may be differences in the *content* put into ideas of these different kinds. That means, if we are talking about right and wrong, that there are different beliefs and interpretations about *what conduct* is right and what is wrong. If we think that right and wrong can be summed up in rules, different people subscribe to different rules, or put different interpretations on what may appear to be the same rules. 'Do not kill', for example, may or may not be interpreted to rule out abortion or capital punishment or war. If we think in terms of principles, different principles will be salient in different times and places (principles of loyalty, of honour, of chastity, have been enormously important in some human communities and may seem to have faded almost entirely from others). If we think about what makes for a good life, is it achievement, wealth, physical comfort, health, fame, good reputation (the notion of 'celebrity' shows that fame and good reputation are not the same), parenthood, public service? You may have a ready answer, but other people will have other answers. If we think in terms of virtues, is humility a virtue (as it was for Jesus of Nazareth, but emphatically not for Aristotle)? What about aggressiveness (which is often today spoken of as a desirable quality in the worlds of sport and business)?

As some of these examples show, we have to supplement the idea of differences in content with the idea of differences in the salience of certain ideas. To some people, the ideas of right and wrong, of what they have a duty to do or to refrain from doing, may seem to expand to fill most of the available space. Others may think relatively little in terms of duty or wrongdoing, and much more in terms of what is desirable both in their own lives and in that of others. One person may recognise that a certain quality is a virtue (generosity, say) and on occasion be glad that others have that quality, but not give it any large place in her own conduct.

Differences in the content and in the salience of ethical notions are not the only differences of interpretation. There may be less obvious but important differences in how the notions themselves are understood. What do 'right' and 'wrong' even mean? This is not the place to catalogue the answers that moral philosophers have given to that question. Perhaps non-philosophers are more likely to ask questions such as 'where do values come from?' 'Are there fundamental values that are rooted in human nature?' 'Are there absolute God-given values?' Or 'Are all values relative to place and time and human preference?' We could say that such questions are about the *source* or *foundation* of values. People can disagree on such questions as these even if they do not disagree on what would be right or good here and now – that the torturing and degradation of prisoners is wrong, say.

The point of mentioning these questions here is not to answer them (that would need a different kind of book – e.g. Blackburn 2001) but to point out that the questions themselves, and the many answers that would be offered to them, are all part of the ethical environment in which we live. That is not a trivial point; the fact that we do not all agree on the answers to such questions is itself an important fact about our ethical environment.

If we focus on the great variety of kinds of idea that are part of our ethical environment, the possibilities of putting different content into any of them, and, even when we agree about content, the possibility that is still open for different interpretations of the meaning and sources of our values, the wonder might be that we find as much agreement as we do. The possible permutations of the different kinds of ideas, where ideas of each kind can carry differences in content, meaning, beliefs about source, and so on, would appear to be vast. But that is to look at the ethical environment as if it were just a set of ideas detached from everything else, equally open to any of the vast number of permutations that, mathematically, would be possible. In fact, of course, human beings inhabit all the other overlapping kinds of environment already mentioned – political, social and so on – within a physical environment that constrains what is possible and probable. Explanations can be given as to why, in the light of some more or less common factors in human life, the variation in values is less than it could theoretically be. Some sorts of prohibition on killing and injuring, some sorts of regulation of truth telling, and so on, are to be expected. Even the difference between naturalistic explanations and religious explanations of where our values 'come from' need not lead us to expect completely different sets of values. Both naturalistic science and theology are likely to expect *some* degree of coherence and fit between the natural environment, human life and values.

Such considerations would lead us to expect *some* agreement on values – on right and wrong conduct, on what ways of life are desirable, on what qualities are admirable, and so on – between any two human individuals taken at random. But that is, of course, a very artificial way of looking at the extent of agreement. The possible permutations of ethical ideas are not randomly distributed across individuals. Each individual shares a lot with some people, and rather less with some others. That is, there is a clustering effect. When we speak of different cultures having different values, or when we think of a certain climate of values in a particular country, we are recognising and labelling some of these clustering effects. We need to look further at the nature of these 'clusters' before we concentrate on ideas about values education.

Culture

Why do ethical ideas come in clusters? One reason, though not the most powerful, is that human beings, as rational animals, have some susceptibility to considerations of consistency and coherence. Not all possible sets of ethical ideas, when the interpretation is filled in, can logically hang together. Yet historical hindsight shows how much individuals and even whole societies can tolerate contradiction in their own principles and practices, such as the contradiction between the principle that 'all men are created equal, that they are endowed by their Creator with certain unalienable Rights, that among these are Life, Liberty and the pursuit of Happiness' and the practice of slavery. Historical explanations are often grounded ultimately in the social nature of human beings rather than their rational capacities. When animals that have ideas cluster together, their ideas will naturally cluster together too. Ethical ideas emerge that help to hold a group together and regulate its activities; the size of the group within which this happens has always within human history, until very recent times, been less than the whole of humanity.

Compared with other animals, a relatively small part of human behaviour is instinctive. Ethical ideas, as well as much else, have to be learned. Education, in the informal sense that starts with early upbringing, is always an initiation first into the *immediate* environment of ideas. What else could it be? Whatever we may think about the possibilities or limitations of autonomy (an idea we shall return to in Chapters 3 and 5), any autonomy vis-à-vis the surrounding environment of ideas cannot come at the beginning of a child's life. Any particular environment of ideas has a tendency to perpetuate itself; it draws people into it, even while some may criticise it, move out of it, or contribute to changing it.

It goes with being social animals, and also with being very dependent when young, that human beings value a sense of belonging, and tend to identify with some group. This is a human tendency that presumably was present long before anyone explicitly drew attention to it, and that seems to be not much affected by the fact that we can now explicitly reflect on it. To belong to a group and to identify with it is, in part, to share its values.

Then, as well (and perhaps this goes with being rational, language-using animals more than with being social) we have a tendency to categorise and label. Contemporary use of the term 'culture' certainly seems to reflect this, perhaps most of all when it is used to mark very broad categories: categories so broad, that is, that their number might be no more than a few score, perhaps even less than a dozen, for the whole world. Such a categorisation at its broadest is illustrated by Kymlicka's remark that 'using "culture" in the widest sense, we can say that all of the Western democracies share a common "culture" – that is, they all share a modern, urban, secular industrialised civilization, in contrast to the feudal, agricultural, and theocratic world of our ancestors' (Kymlicka 1995: 18).

Suppose we use the term 'Culture', with an upper case C, for very broad groupings. How do we in fact, in common parlance, differentiate Cultures? By associating a Culture with one of several other factors – none of which is directly and explicitly a reference to values. Sometimes culture is confused with ethnicity, which is itself a slippery term. We can only make a clear distinction between culture and ethnicity if we restrict the term 'ethnicity' to what is biologically given, encoded in DNA. But then it ought to be obvious that logically there is no necessary connection between ethnicity and culture, simply because culture has to be learned (this is part of the definition of 'culture', not just in human contexts but also in the study of other species). We can invent a use for a term such as 'black culture', but to assume that one can identify someone's membership of a certain sort of culture from the colour of their skin would be no more defensible than any other racial stereotyping. So, despite the fact that 'multicultural' and 'multiethnic', and even 'multiracial' are sometimes used interchangeably (even in academic writing), one place where it would be better to draw a sharp line is between the categories of culture and of ethnicity.

Sometimes a Culture is identified by reference to geography. A category such as 'Chinese culture' is better understood by reference to the history, language and customs of the people of a geographical region than by reference to ethnicity. (Ethnically Chinese people born and brought up in other parts of the world may not share in a Chinese culture.) Related to but not the same as geographical classification is the association of culture with nationality: Spanish culture, South African culture and so on. It hardly needs saying that 'nation' and 'nationality' are socially constructed and rather fluid categories.

Then there is classification by religion: Hindu culture, Islamic culture, and so on. This is not immune from confusion with geographical categorisation, as in the not uncommon perception of a tension between 'Western' and 'Islamic'. Samuel Huntington (2002), in his terminology of 'Civilizations' rather than 'Cultures', mixed geographical and religious markers on his listing of civilisations which he predicted would increasingly clash: not just

Western and Islamic, but Latin American, African, Japanese and Chinese, Hindu, Orthodox and Buddhist.

There is a constant danger of oversimplification in using such large-scale categorisations, because it can lead us to overlook concrete complexity. Any Culture, identified in a broad-brush way, will be very diverse in its internal composition. Waldron, in something approaching a general definition, says that

> the culture of a community is a way of doing things, particularly the things that are done *together*, throughout the whole course of human life: language, governance, religious rituals, rites of passage, family structures, material production and decoration, economy, science, warfare, and the sharing of a sense of history.
>
> Waldron 1996: 96

We can add values and ethical ideas and beliefs, recognising that these are not distinct elements from those mentioned by Waldron, but variously embodied in the different aspects of discourse and practice he mentions. In any of the categories mentioned there is scope for change across time and variation from place to place (differences of dialect, different historical stories, doctrinal divisions within one religion, different interpretations of ethical principles, and so on). When a community is fairly small and actually living together in one place, then all the elements of its culture may at least *appear* to form a seamless whole; but when the ideas and practices of a culture are no longer closely attached to one community in one place, it is all the more likely that diverse elements of the culture will develop in different ways.

In relation to individuals, we noted above the problem of integration that can arise when different elements of the ethical environment are in tension. The same can be true of cultures. Just as the varying kinds of ethical considerations have to be held together in an individual life, so within a culture ideas have to hold together, and the culture ceases to exist if there is too much pulling apart. On the other hand, the dangers of disintegration of a culture because of conflicting strands within it may be less than the dangers of disintegration for an individual. Cultures have various dimensions of continuity, and a shared sense of history, shared language, shared values may hold a culture together in the face of large disagreements (commitment to some values may even hold it together in the face of disagreement over other values). One of the ethically pertinent questions to ask about a culture is, indeed, how resilient it is to internal disagreement.

The internal heterogeneity of cultures makes interpenetration between cultures possible: a person may share in the sense of history of one culture, speak a language that had its origins in another culture, believe in a religion that had its origins in yet another culture, and so on. In the modern world a person who may identify primarily with one culture can also know a lot about another: the ideas of one culture can be available for use more widely, to the extent that within a multicultural society an individual may form her own sense of identity out of a mix of cultural elements (Waldron 1996). It is vital that schooling both recognises this possibility and helps individuals who are trying to do this.

Ideas about the clustering of values within cultures and about cultural difference are themselves part of our ethical environment. But such ideas can be hard to interpret if it is not clear whether the notion of culture is being used in the broad upper-case C way or in one of the much finer-grained ways in which we can use the word (Kymlicka 1995: 18). Take the question 'why should we tolerate competing ethical cultures that threaten us, and that seem to us pernicious?'[5] If the sense of culture intended in this question is Culture, one of those large categories holding to some degree the identification and allegiance of many millions of people, then the idea that a whole Culture can be pernicious (and that the question of tolerating it even arises – see Chapter 4 below) is disturbing. It makes a sweeping generalisation (since it is hard to see how such a loose-knit conglomeration could in its entirety be pernicious) and taints by association a multitude of individuals who will have been born and brought up into that Culture. If, on the other hand, a much more specific focus is intended, then probably every reader can think of cultures he or she would judge pernicious. Examples might be Ku Klux Klan culture in the USA, neo-Nazi culture in parts of Europe, an international internet-based culture of paedophilia, and the cultures of terrorist organisations or groupings, in various parts of the world, that will subordinate all other considerations to the pursuit of their ends by violent means.

A question might be raised here as to what the standpoint is from which an ethical judgement about a culture can be made. It will be argued in Chapter 4 that while it is true that there is no standpoint external to the ethical environment from which we can evaluate any part of that environment, that by no means makes our judgements groundless. For the rest of this chapter, the task is to pursue the idea of culture with a lower-case c as an aspect of the ethical environment.

Dimensions of culture

Rather than draw boundaries around distinct cultures, it is better to recognise broad dimensions along which ethical ideas and the salience given to those ideas can vary. This is better not only because it is more accurate, but also because in education it is likely to be fairer to individuals. While cultural identity needs to be recognised within education, that is a different matter from categorising people in broad groupings without recognising the cross-cutting variations.

At least one of these broad dimensions has become so much a part of thinking about culture well beyond the bounds of academic research that it is itself a salient part of many people's perceptions of the ethical environment. This is the continuum from maximum emphasis on the individual to maximum emphasis on the community: in shorthand, the individualism–collectivism dimension. As a dimension along which cultural differences are found this has some fairly weighty empirical support (Hofstede 1980; Smith and Bond 1993). As a heuristic device it can help us to organise our thinking about cultural variation and to make sense of a number of other dimensions that researchers have identified. Among these is another identified by Hofstede (1991): 'Power-Distance', which refers to the distance between those with power (or perceived authority) and those subordinate to them. At one end of this spectrum, there is an expectation of clear direction from those in authority, and a corresponding deference from subordinates, who see themselves as members of the collective (a firm, an organisation, a nation) first, and individuals second; at the other end, with greater emphasis on individual identity, an expectation of relative equality, consultation and involvement.

Some social anthropologists, going back to Benedict (1946), have distinguished *shame* cultures and *guilt* cultures. In a shame culture, the avoidance of shame or the pursuit of honour are strong motivations for acting according to the norms. Shame, honour and dishonour are rooted in how a person is seen by others. The flourishing of the group is valued above the flourishing of the individual, and to the extent that the individual identifies with the group, the group's sense of what is right and proper will be motivations for her also. In a guilt culture the emphasis is on individual right action. A person will feel guilty when she has done what she perceives as immoral (or know she would feel guilty if she did it), though she believes no one else ever will know about it. Consider the difference between 'I couldn't look other people in the face if I did that' and 'I couldn't live with myself if I did that'. Both can be motivating, but one is outward looking, one inward looking.

While this is a real distinction, it does not follow that it will serve in the modern world to mark any sharp boundaries between cultures. Honour killings (killings believed to be required in order to uphold a family's honour) are not unknown in developed Western societies – among people, that is, who share in at least some aspects of the wider culture of those societies. As the example from everyday English above suggests, reactions and anticipations both of shame and of guilt may be possible for the same people.

Some psychologists (beginning with Gilligan 1982) have distinguished different ethical orientations or perspectives that are variously labelled 'justice' and 'caring' or 'separateness' and 'connectedness'. Within a justice orientation a person deciding what to do will make considerations of justice primary; often this means focusing on individual rights. Would I be within my rights to do such-and-such (even though I don't *have* to do this, and the consequences will be bad for others if I do?). Within the same orientation, when two people are in dispute, the expectation will be that one will turn out to have right on his or her side; the important question is which person that is. Broad-brush considerations are being brought in from outside and applied to the particular case. A 'caring' (Noddings 1984) or 'connectedness' orientation, in contrast, does not expect to get the right answer in this way; or, we could say, it does not expect that the *right* answer in terms of individual's rights will necessarily be the *best* answer to the concrete problem. It looks for the best answer by seeking in the actual situation for the best available outcome for all concerned, putting particular emphasis on the maintaining where possible of ongoing relationships.

This seems to be a sufficiently strong distinction that it might mark a division between cultures. But in fact the available research suggests that if anything it represents not a cultural difference but a gender difference. Males to some extent, it seems, are more likely to take the justice orientation, females the caring orientation. But that is at most a tendency, and may reflect differences in the upbringing of boys and girls that cut across cultures as characterised earlier. Both males and females seem to be capable of appreciating and working within both orientations. Educationally, there are strong reasons for trying to see that both boys and girls become able to appreciate both orientations, and able to work within both: this will both enhance individuals' understanding of the ways in which others are thinking, and make it more likely that they will bring the most appropriate orientation to the situations they face (Haydon 1997: 138–139). For it may well be both that different orientations are appropriate to different kinds of situation or issue, and that the difference between the orientations is not as clear-cut as has sometimes been thought (Dancy 1992; Katz *et al.* 1999).

The culture of schools

Our initial characterisation of an ethical environment was 'the surrounding climate of ideas about how to live'. Once we have recognised that the notion of 'culture' has to be treated as fluid, we can see that the notion of a climate of ideas about how to live is at no great distance from it. Indeed we might have expected this from the fact that in the context of schools it is not easy to distinguish 'school climate' from 'school culture' (Glover and Coleman 2005). Perhaps we will more naturally speak of 'a climate of ideas' or 'climate of values' when we are thinking of a tendency that has no long history behind it, no roots in a specific community or specific place, and which may turn out to be more ephemeral. In the British context, for instance, commentators now refer to the individualistic 'me-first' climate that was engendered (or at any rate encouraged) by the Thatcher government in the 1980s, and the same commentators will occasionally think that a somewhat more caring climate has emerged since then. Certainly there seems now to be more talk of ethics within business than there used to be. Yet at the same time the entrepreneurial, target-driven, even profit-driven climate that Ball (2003) identified has become much stronger in education under New Labour than it was under Thatcher.

In a context of values, whether we speak of culture, climate or environment, we are interested in such questions as the weight and ranking that is given to certain values, which values appear actually to be most salient at a given time, the way those values are interpreted, what is considered to be acceptable or unacceptable, praiseworthy or blameworthy, and whether anything is considered to be obligatory or absolutely ruled out. In the context of educational management, for instance, someone might say that economic efficiency is being elevated while trust in teacher professionalism is being eroded; in the process the interpretation of trust changes, from being personal trust that a community might place in its teachers, to being trust in a system because its outcomes will be assured if everyone follows the rules. Head teachers are praised if they can move their school up the league tables, while a certain amount of manipulation of the figures may be considered acceptable, not blameworthy; it may even become a moot point for teachers themselves whether cheating is ruled out if it seems to serve the school's purposes (Davies 2000). The truth of such a description may, of course, be disputed; it serves here as an illustration of what it means to talk about a changing climate, or culture, or ethical environment within the world of schooling. Exactly which term we use is not a major issue. But as I suggested in the previous chapter, to speak of the ethical environment may fit more readily with the idea that we all live in a global ethical environment, while we also inhabit more specific environments that show differences.

Some constituents of the global ethical environment

We can conclude this chapter with a brief review of some of the commonalities that may be found within that global environment. First, then, what were identified in the first part of this chapter as the various constituents of the ethical environment – the different kinds of evaluation in which we are interested, and the different kinds of object that we evaluate – will cut across local environments. Everywhere there is likely to be some recognition of certain general moral expectations or rules of conduct. This does not mean that the recognition will always be more than lip service, or that every individual will attach weight to what are seen as moral rules in his or her environment. And it does not mean that the content of the rules will always be the same. But it does in fact seem possible to find quite wide agreement on content at a level that is admittedly not very precise. Perhaps the clearest example lies in the idea of human rights. This has, of course, been consciously promoted in recent times, through the United Nations Universal Declaration of Human Rights and through other international agencies including the European Union. The discourse of human rights provides both a vocabulary that all are capable of using (to the extent and with the interpretation that they wish) and a degree of consensus, whether honoured in the observance or the breach, on content.

Everywhere also there is likely to be recognition of some personal qualities as desirable and admirable. There is room for variation as to which qualities these are. Some philosophers (notably MacIntyre 1981) have drawn attention to the way in which particular conceptions of virtues will be rooted in shared traditions, so that there will be different lists and interpretations of virtues within different traditions. But this does not rule out a degree of consensus on at least some qualities as being desirable. Carr (2003: 231) suggests, on the basis of cross-cultural recognition of such qualities as integrity, honesty and courage, that 'the language of virtue is arguably the cross-cultural ethical currency of humankind'.

Everywhere people will have some stock of understandings, shared with others around them to a greater or lesser extent, of what makes for a good life. The theoretical room for variation here is vast (since every way of life which human beings have ever followed anywhere on the planet must be a *possible* way of life, and it is unlikely that all the possibilities have been exhausted; indeed changing technology is making new possibilities available). But in practice it is part of the relatively modern and increasingly strong set of tendencies we call *globalisation* that there comes to be more convergence in ways of life. Kymlicka's description of the culture of Western democracies as 'modern, urban, secular industrialised civilization' becomes increasingly – for better or worse – to be not that only of the West. More controversially, the same may be true of the materialism and consumerism that arguably is part of this civilization. But the awareness that this is not the only way to live is still very strong, and perhaps one element especially of that characterisation – the secularity – has never swept all before it and may even be in retreat.

We might add that a recognition of the ethical importance of education is itself a widely shared strand of the ethical environment, while more specific conceptions of specialised areas of education such as moral education, citizenship education or character education may have special salience within different environments. The next chapter will begin to look in more detail at ideas of the role of education within the ethical environment.

3 Conceptions of values education

What should education be doing in the area of values? I mean by this, not 'How should education proceed?', but 'What should education be aiming at? What should it be trying to achieve? What would count as success?' My concern here will be primarily with what is done deliberately in schools, and since I want these questions about educational aims to be understood throughout in relation to values I shall, as I explained in the Introduction, use 'values education' as a shorthand, but without presupposing any particular answer as to whether there should be a distinct part of the curriculum or timetable that should be dealing with values, or, if there is to be such an area, what it should be called.

One of the tasks of a philosopher in relation to values education is to focus on the question of aims. A philosopher will not – and should not, with any claim to authority – try to tell practitioners just what they should be doing in the classroom, or indeed to tell policy-makers exactly what their policy should be. But the philosopher can reasonably take the view that reflection on the aims of the activity can improve the quality of the activity. At its most dramatic, careful reflection on the aims of values education could avoid teachers and policy-makers putting their time and energy into something that would be better not done at all (because, for example, it might be indoctrinatory in some subtle way); more probably in practice and more prosaically, where teachers are already engaged in some activity that is worth pursuing, and that is conducted under the label of values education or something related to that, they are likely to do it more effectively if they are clear about what it is they are aiming at.

In this chapter I shall discuss a variety of conceptions of values education, distinguished chiefly by their different aims. I shall not claim to have exhausted all the possible conceptions of values education; I concentrate on some that are not just possible but actually subscribed to with more or less reflection by considerable numbers of people. At the end of the chapter I shall add to the list two linked suggestions that draw directly on the idea of the ethical environment.

Educational ideas as part of the ethical environment

There are two reasons for concentrating on values education only after a broader survey of the idea of the ethical environment and its constituents, in all its diversity. First, conceptions of values education – indeed, conceptions more generally of what education is about and why it is worthwhile, and more generally still, conceptions of the proper relationship between adults and children – are themselves aspects of the ethical environment. Think of ideas such as 'children should be seen and not heard'; or 'we want children to grow up able to think for themselves'; or 'the most important thing at school is that children should be happy' or 'children should be brought up to be productive members of society'. Or recall from the last chapter Hofstede's Power-Distance dimension. In the context of schooling, the idea that children should be brought up to show obedience and deference towards their elders would be towards one end of this dimension, the idea that parents and teachers should encourage children to be critical and exercise their own initiative would be towards the other end. Then too there are prevailing ideas, differing in different societies, about what methods of discipline are appropriate with children, and about how far children as they grow up should be expected to care for their aging parents. All such ideas, informally stated as they are, express or depend on thoughts about the responsibilities of adults towards children, about the responsibilities that children will come to have as they grow up, about what is important in life, about the nature of a good society.

The second reason for looking in detail at ideas about values education only after looking at the constituents of the ethical environment is that the variety of extant ideas about values education to some degree corresponds to the variety of constituents within the ethical environment that we have already looked at. All formal education is, in part, a continuation of the socialisation by which individuals are inducted into their surrounding culture, where 'culture', in line with the arguments of the last chapter, is not meant to imply a discrete or homogeneous entity. One way of approaching the idea of values education more specifically is to think of it as an induction into the ethical aspects of the surrounding culture – which is to say, in effect, the immediate ethical environment. But this so far leaves almost everything still to be said about which aspects of that environment are to be emphasised or what view of the interrelationships between the various aspects of the ethical environment is to be embodied within education. If we emphasise moral rules, we may see values education as the teaching of the rules; if we emphasise virtues, we will see the development of virtues as the important thing, and so on. The fact that our ethical environment does contain this variety of constituents should act as a warning that putting all the weight on some particular set of ideas may be to take too narrow a view of values education.

Social and individual aims

If we use the individualist/collectivist dimension as a useful heuristic, then we can recognise first that individualist and collectivist aims (or, simply, individual and social aims) can be compatible within one education system. Any society will want its young people to grow up in ways that contribute to the flourishing of the society, or that at least do not damage it. Parents *may* share these aims for the good of the society, but they may also wish what is best for their own children. And the whole society *may* be committed, not just to promoting the overall benefit of society, but to promoting the well-being of each individual child. That this should be an aim of education pursued by the state, not just by the parents of individual children, is a tenet of modern liberal-democratic thinking (cf. Brighouse 2000, 2006). Where the overall well-being of each individual child is the aim, education can hardly assume in advance that any aspect of the ethical environment will turn out to be irrelevant. Where the aim is the flourishing of society, it will become clear that the same is the case. But in practice it is not surprising if a concern with the good of society has often led to a rather narrower focus, which is a focus on *morality*, if morality is conceived as having to do with how individuals behave towards each other. The focus of both academic literature and public concern has often, then, been on *moral* education (which is still, as we shall see, open to a variety of interpretations).

If a society's aims focus on behaviour, in the hope that people's behaviour will be beneficial to others or at least not anti-social, then it is likely that what will offer itself as the most direct way of influencing behaviour is the promulgation of rules that tell people what to do and what not to do. This is, of course, one thing that legal systems attempt to do, but it can also be done in more informal ways. We are then in the territory of that law-like conception of *morality in the narrow sense* to which I referred in the last chapter. Within this conception, one task of schools will be to teach children the rules of morality. On the face of it, there is an advantage in schools, within a common state system, rather than parents or local communities, taking on this role: they can ensure that the same rules are taught to everyone. That in turn ensures that people will not have radically different expectations about each other's behaviour, so that reliability and the possibilities for cooperation are enhanced.

It is not only within a collectivist view that someone may think that schools should be teaching moral rules. Parents who have their children's best interests at heart may want them to follow accepted rules because life is likely to be more difficult for them if they do not (Hare 1981: Ch. 11). And if parents think that the rules of morality are not just the accepted conventions of society but have some more objective or absolute status, they may think, independently of the consequences for society, that their children will not be leading a good life if they do not follow the rules.

The aim of inculcating rule following, however, whether it is taken for individualist or collectivist reasons, cannot be adequate by itself. The chief reason for this is that any set of rules that is sufficiently general to be laid down in advance will not be sufficiently determinate to give detailed guidance in all the twists and turns of life. Sometimes, as we saw in the previous chapter, rules can conflict (for example, 'tell the truth' and 'don't hurt people' in a case where telling the truth will be hurtful); even where there is no direct conflict, rules (which are often negative, telling people what *not* to do) will not give precise guidance on what *is* to be done. Somehow, when the rules are not sufficiently determinate, people have to be able to find out what to do in particular circumstances.

How are they to find out? There are some answers that might be unlikely to occur to people within an individualist environment. One such is: 'Ask someone else who is more likely to know', someone who is older, more experienced and wiser (Hursthouse 1999: 35). Children could perhaps be taught to do this, and taught how to recognise such people. In environments in which there is a high degree of respect and deference to elders, and in religious environments in which there are priests or spiritual advisers, that may still seem a good answer. Theoretically, of course, it only pushes the question back one stage, since we could still ask how the older and wiser person is to know. And in practice it has severe limitations as an answer, since people have to live their lives from day to day going through situations in which it is not always possible to search for guidance from someone else.

Another answer that may have force within certain kinds of tradition is to follow the example of a specific person, who is not around to be asked face-to-face but who is present in history, religious faith or myth. It is reported from the United States that some Christians with a sense of responsibility for the natural environment are asking 'What kind of car would Jesus have driven?' The question is too narrow (since, to enter into the spirit of the question, one would have to consider that Jesus might have relied on public transport) but the main problem with the question is again that it only pushes the question back one stage, since it is the environmentalists here and now who have to decide what the answer is.

Teaching ethical thinking

In the real world, then, we can hardly get away from saying that people will have to be able, at least in cases where there are no sufficiently determinate rules, to think for themselves, to exercise their own judgement. One way of following up this point is to say that education should aim to develop *autonomy*. The idea of autonomy, however, needs further interpretation. At one extreme, it is not uncommon in liberal environments to come across the insufficiently considered idea that individuals should ultimately choose their own values. That will not do, for at least two reasons. The most obvious is that society has an interest in individuals *not* making certain choices, such as choosing completely to disregard the interests of others. Less obvious is that the notion of individuals choosing all of their own values is incoherent. I cannot make any specific choice without taking something, at least at that time, as a basis on which to compare one possibility with another. If everything all the time is considered to be up for choice, I cannot make anything that can count as a choice – rather than arbitrary drifting – at all. The actual possibility of choice, then, depends on an initial induction into some ethical environment, from which standards can be taken, though those same standards may at some point be criticised and rejected (more will be said in the next chapter on how this is possible). If there could be no basis for adherence to any values beyond an arbitrary drifting towards this or that there would be no basis for any development of autonomy.

It *is* a possible interpretation of autonomy to say that individuals should be able, in time, to endorse for themselves the values they hold. That is close to the idea, to which I shall return, that individuals need to be able to find their own way through the ethical environment. But for the moment we need to look at what is involved in a person thinking for herself in specific circumstances. Teachers often want students to think for themselves. At a minimum this may simply mean 'working out the answer, not looking it up in the back of the book', or 'doing your own work, not copying from the person next to you'. Pushing this slightly further, teachers will want their students to do some thinking that goes beyond that they have actually been told, by the teacher or the textbook: to do a little historical or mathematical or scientific thinking of their own. But this clearly does not imply that the students can do whatever kind of thinking they like: the teacher will hope that what they do is the right kind of thinking, *appropriate* to history or mathematics or science. Similarly, if we want people to develop the capacity to think for themselves on questions of right and wrong, good and bad, this does not mean that just any way of thinking will do. In some sense we will want to teach them *how* to think about such matters.[1]

One popular demand that turns out to be unhelpful is that schools should teach children *the difference between right and wrong*. This can be understood in several ways. One is that children must be taught what kinds of behaviour are right, what kinds of behaviour are wrong. This is the sort of task that sounds as if it could be performed by giving children a list and making sure that they learn it. (A comparison might be 'teaching children to distinguish fruit from vegetables'. Perhaps at some point in the teaching of young children they might be presented with two lists. Bananas and oranges would come on the list headed 'fruit'; potatoes and yams on the list headed 'vegetables'. Later they will learn on what basis the distinction is made.) But on this interpretation teaching the difference between right and wrong is just another way of laying down rules, and is no more satisfactory.

Another interpretation is that children need, not just to be able to classify actions under 'right' and 'wrong' but to *care* about which is which; what is right needs to have some positive motivational weight for them, and what is wrong a negative weight. That is one way of making a vital point that we shall have to come back to later: that education relating to morality cannot be just a cognitive matter but must involve feeling and motivation.

Though it cannot be just a cognitive matter, the cognitive question is still to be answered: how are people to tell what is right and what is wrong? One strategy here would be to suggest that everyone should try to follow the example of certain philosophers who have believed that there is a rational strategy by which answers to moral questions can eventually be derived from one supreme principle. In the past few centuries of moral philosophy there have been two main theories of this kind. One was briefly mentioned in the last chapter: utilitarianism, which holds that the ultimate criterion of what is right and good is the achievement of the greatest possible balance of happiness over unhappiness for all concerned. Putting to one side for the moment the fact that many people feel this is *not* what morality is ultimately about, there is a question about what kind of decision-making procedure follows from this ultimate criterion. It does not follow that everyone on every occasion should try to decide what would be the right thing to do purely by considering what would have the best consequences in the particular circumstances that face them. If everyone did this, the actual consequences might be chaotic. We noted above the advantages for reliability and cooperation if everyone follows the same rules. If all we know about the way other people will behave is that they will do whatever seems likely to them at the time to have the best consequences, then we will not know what they will do; and, of course, anyone's judgement about what will have the best consequences may turn out to be mistaken. Such difficulties explain why most utilitarians have been considerably more subtle in their recommendations. There may be better consequences all round if people follow certain set rules, or if they acquire certain entrenched virtues, or if they make their decisions on some other basis altogether. So yet again, the question about how people should make their judgements of what to do has only been pushed back.

The other major theory that claims a rational basis for right and wrong in one overriding criterion is the ethics of Immanuel Kant. For Kant (1785), there is always a way in which you can test whether something you are proposing to do is morally acceptable: roughly, you must see if you can, without falling into any contradiction, subscribe to a universal principle that would allow everyone to act in the way you are proposing. For instance, if you are considering whether it is all right, for your own convenience, to make a promise that you know you cannot keep, you must consider whether it could be a universal principle that anyone may for their own convenience make a promise that they know they cannot keep. For Kant, there is a contradiction in the very idea of a universal principle to this effect; therefore, rationally, it cannot be acceptable for you to make an exception for yourself in acting that way.

This is already avoiding many of the complexities of what is a very subtle chain of reasoning in Kant. He was not proposing this test of universalisability as something he just happened to have dreamt up; rather he thought that, if we once accept that we are rational animals, capable of following reason and free to act accordingly, then reason compels us to accept that we must not act in ways that cannot be universalised. He also argued that there were other ways of expressing that fundamental principle (or 'categorical imperative'). One of his alternative formulations comes quite close to the idea of 'respect for persons', which some commentators (e.g. Downie and Telfer 1969) have seen as Kant's main legacy in ethics. This formulation has it that we should treat other individuals as 'ends in themselves'; that is, we should never treat another *purely* as a means to our own ends.

The very subtlety and ingenuity of Kant's argument, including his reasons for treating his various formulations of the categorical imperative as equivalent, may call into doubt whether education should attempt to teach Kant's own theory as a basis for everyone's moral judgement. At the level of professional education, for instance in ethics courses for student doctors and nurses, these theories, sometimes in watered-down and not entirely accurate versions, have often been explicitly taught (Beauchamp and Childress 1989, more accurate than many, has been through many editions as one of the major texts). But in what sense do they give guidance? One philosopher has commented that by these 'courses in comparative ethical theory' we produce 'persons who have been convinced by our teaching that whatever they do in some difficult situation, some moral theory will condone it, another will condemn it' (Baier 1985: 208).

If that is a fair assessment of the situation in professional ethics, it is understandable that few writers have advocated the explicit teaching of philosophical theories of ethics as part of values education at school level. But it may be that something that is philosophically of lighter weight, and even eclectic, may still have a place (Haydon 2000a). Giving some weight to consequences is, as noted in the last chapter, part of our everyday thinking about what to do; and the classic Golden Rule 'do to others as you would have them do to you' is not entirely unrelated to Kant's theory. Several approaches to values education (including Hare 1992 and Kohlberg 1981 in his formulation of Stage 6 reasoning) have given central place to some version of universalisability (Kohlberg called his version 'reversability'), while recognising that using such a test may actually require us to look at consequences (as the formulation 'what if everyone did that?' suggests). But this does not mean that there is any single metric by which to assess whether consequences are good or bad.

Recognising the complexity of the ethical environment

At this point we are coming back from the kind of ethical theory that subordinates all moral questions to one overriding criterion, towards the more complex texture of the actual ethical environment as we experience it. There are *many* things that matter to us, and we may simply have to accept this fact without supposing that all the things that matter will fit neatly together, and without looking for an overriding theory to resolve all doubts. This is a recognition of *pluralism* in a sense that has no essential connection with plurality of cultures. We are talking now about a plurality of *values* that we can appreciate even within one culture (however we delineate that). Isaiah Berlin (1990, 1997, 2000) devoted much of his work to defending the view that political judgement must recognise a plurality of goods. These include liberty and equality, which no political theory has ever managed convincingly to collapse together, and to these we can add such values as material welfare and, importantly but less tangibly, respect for identity and difference. The plurality of values is equally present in personal life. For instance, surveying the constituents of the ethical environment in the last chapter, I mentioned values of honesty, loyalty and trustworthiness that may all have to be weighed up in particular circumstances and that may sometimes pull in different directions.

If there are many values that need to be recognised, then a central task of values education will be to help people to come to an awareness of these values, and *to take them into account in their lives.* What will this mean? To answer this we have to leave the survey of cognitive approaches and come back to a vital point already mentioned but deferred: that values education must involve feeling and motivation. People can hardly be said to *have* certain values if they do not care about these values: honesty, loyalty, trustworthiness and so on have to matter to them (to interpret 'and so on' you can write in whatever values matter most to you). And their caring about these values has to be able to translate into action.

Pursuing this line of thought is one route by which many theorists of values education have moved away from concentrating on principles (let alone rules) towards a focus on virtues (Carr and Steutel 1999). It is not that having a virtue and following principles are mutually exclusive. A person who has developed a range of important virtues will still be able to take into account whatever moral rules and principles are widely recognised within her society. But she will not let any rules or principles be the last word in determining her conduct, and often she will not be explicitly following any rules or principles at all. This may be in part because she has, in acquiring a particular virtue, fully internalised a certain principle (this helps explain why we can often use the same word, such as 'honesty', to identify a principle that can be followed, or a state of character that someone displays). But she may also (some virtue theorists would say) not be following principles at all (even internalised ones) because the ethical features of actual situations are just too complex and uncodifiable to be captured by any set of principles.[2]

Consistently with this, the virtue theorist can be a pluralist about values, recognising that there can be many goods. It is good for suffering to be relieved, and good that people be treated fairly, but we cannot just assume that the two goods can always fit together. Similarly we cannot just assume that the virtue of benevolence, and the virtue of justice (which we can ascribe to a person who has a strong sense of justice, cares about justice and tries to realise it in practice) can fit neatly together in one person and one life. But some people do think that all virtues can fit together, and even that a person cannot genuinely have one virtue without having them all: a notion sometimes labelled 'the unity of virtues'. The point is much debated among philosophers of virtue (Hursthouse 1999: 153–157).

Having a virtue certainly does not rule out thinking hard about what to do. If virtue theorists are right, the virtuous person will be as capable as anyone else of reflecting on what to do in particular circumstances, and her answers will be ones which take into account the complexities of reality, rather than trying, as it were, to make reality fit some predetermined principles, or to go through some predetermined process of reasoning. If that is so, then rather than seeing a virtue approach to values education as an alternative to other approaches we may be able to see it as a comprehensive approach that can offer the best of all the rest and more (Haydon 2003). But we clearly cannot leave the matter there, since the virtue theorist owes us some account of how the virtuous person decides what to do. Is there some special capacity involved that the virtuous person has and other people do not? And if there is, can it be taught? Something will be said on those questions below in the context of the relationship between virtues and the ethical environment.

It is worth noting here that when we think of values education as a matter of developing virtues it becomes more nearly continuous with the whole of education, whereas rules or principles, or specific ways of thinking to be engaged in when there are moral decisions to be made, may seem to be the focus of some special part of education. That focus within education may correspond to a more general way of thinking about ethics: that it only impinges on certain episodes of a person's life. Such a focus in turn fits well with a certain liberal way of thinking by which people's choices about how to live their own lives fall largely outside the scope of ethics, provided certain basic moral constraints are respected. But the view of the ethical environment that we took in the last chapter incorporated much more than basic constraints. It included all those value-laden ideas about what is worthwhile in life, what makes for a good life, that are relevant to people's own choices about how to live their lives. What a person thinks is worthwhile, what she cares about, what she finds enjoyable, what she appreciates in the world around her, what she would be willing to give up for something more important, what she might in the end be unwilling to do – these are all factors that will enter into the quality of her life, and equally are factors that make her the kind of person she is. It is hard, then, to separate the two questions: 'What sort of person is it good to be?' and 'What sort of life is it good to live?' Certainly within education any attempt to discuss or to answer these two questions in different parts of the curriculum would be artificial.

This discussion of values education has proceeded so far by separating out certain conceptions of its aims: that values education is about teaching rules; about teaching people to think for themselves (which might be by the utilitarian or the Kantian criterion), or about developing virtues. It is important to see that values education, according to any of these conceptions, is likely to depend for its success on the quality of the ethical environment in which the education takes place.

The importance of the ethical environment in values education

When values education is seen as a matter of teaching certain rules, or certain determinate conceptions of what is right or what is wrong, it is usually taken for granted that these rules or notions of right and wrong are already present in the wider ethical environment. The 'wider ethical environment' here will not necessarily be the whole society; a faith school may, for instance, be teaching certain rules of conduct that are not shared outside the faith. But these will still be rules recognised by a community wider than the school, not rules that the school has itself thought up. If the rules that a school is trying to teach are not widely recognised outside the school itself, the teaching is much less likely to be effective.

There is a caveat here: that often a school will have its own rules that regulate the conduct of people within the school for purposes of health, safety or convenience. As Warnock (1977: 138) points out, the cause of values education will not be helped if rules of this sort are confused with moral rules. If a school refers to rules of both kinds, then ensuring that children recognise the difference will be part of the school's educational task. A rule such as 'always walk on the left-hand side of the stairs' has a different status from any moral rule; for one thing, schools often intend their rules of conduct to apply only to students, not to teachers; but a rule could hardly be a moral rule if it did not apply to teachers as well. The success of a rule-based conception of values education will be dependent, then, on the extent to which the rules are recognised and honoured in the surrounding environment, and the detailed content of the education will depend on which rules are recognised within a given community.

Suppose we concentrate instead on the idea of enabling and encouraging people to think for themselves. As noted above, such an aim is sometimes brought under the heading of *autonomy*. It might seem at first sight that the achievement of autonomy as an aim can hardly be dependent on the wider ethical environment, since autonomy is a matter of an individual doing her own thinking and deciding her own action independently of the surrounding environment. But the fact that autonomy is a value favoured in some ethical environments more than in others shows that the environment is relevant after all. In some communities, parents may for the most part want their children to grow up following accepted ways of thinking and acting, with little value attached to the children coming to be independent-minded. In other communities, children may be expected to become independent not just economically but intellectually and emotionally; some parents may think that a degree of rebellion against parental expectations is a normal and even proper part of growing up (that is compatible with never wishing the child to rebel against any specific instruction). Whole societies can vary in the degree to which their social, political and economic arrangements are premised on the exercise of individual autonomy. In a society that expects a greater degree of autonomy, to achieve autonomy may be an important condition of living a good life; but since such a society will also support individual autonomy to a greater degree (e.g. in arrangements that legally embody the rights of young people independently of their parents' rights) it will be correspondingly easier for individuals to achieve autonomy (Raz 1986; White 1991). So both the importance of the aim of individual autonomy, and the likely success in achieving it, are relative to the surrounding ethical environment.

Turning to specific ways in which people may be taught to exercise their thinking on ethical matters, it is clear that utilitarianism, or any variety of consequentialism, has to take the ethical environment into account. Whether the consequences of some action or policy are positive or negative for particular individuals is in part a function of the values which those particular people hold. The world of entertainment provides obvious examples: some music, films and computer games bring great pleasure to some young people and considerable displeasure to their parents. Often we cannot even describe the consequences in any illuminating way without taking values into account. Does a particular action (perhaps swearing in public, or writing graffiti) cause offence? It depends on the values of the perceiver. But that is not to say that the matter is purely subjective. The standards of what is offensive, what is generally considered to be harmless enjoyment, and so on, will be standards that, even if they are not agreed by everyone, are part of the ethical environment. We would find it hard to understand an individual who claims to be offended by something that no one else in her society finds remotely objectionable.

Reasoning based in Kantian ethics may seem to come closest to being independent of the ethical environment. Kantian ethics is often associated with the idea that the individual – any individual of normal rational capacities – is capable of seeing for herself, regardless of what others may think and do, that certain actions are right or wrong. Kant refers to the fundamental principle of ethics as a 'compass' (Kant 1785: 69); a compass is an instrument an individual can use by herself. If I am following a compass and no one else is, then I can be going in the right direction even if everyone else is going in a different direction.

While Kant does see moral reasoning as not having to take the ethical environment into account, this is not, in his view, true of moral education. Kant speaks of giving children examples of people who have stood by their sense of what is right in the face of the indifference or cowardice of others. A modern defender of Kantian ethics (Callender 2004) has cited as an example that might be used in moral education the case of the American woman Erin Brokovich, who in the face of opposition and at great personal cost brought a legal action against the local utility corporation that was contaminating the water supply. The case became widely known through the eponymous film. It is essential to the educational purpose that the case is a real one. If it were purely fiction, it would show young people nothing about the actual possibility of one individual standing up for what she believes to be right against a corporation that has all the power on its side.

As Callender points out, the fact that such a film, and others on similar themes, can be commercially successful illustrates something important about our ethical environment:

> Hollywood makes films intended for mass consumption as a means of making money and there is clearly a great deal of money to be made by holding up a moral ideal in the midst of a society whose general practice tends to run directly counter to it. Given the bottom line to which the eyes of the studios are permanently fixed this could only be so if, despite all evidence to the contrary, there yet remains a certain respect for moral principles and at least an aspiration as to how a person should, morally speaking, conduct themselves.
>
> Callender 2004: 161

If this were not true of our ethical environment, bringing any one individual up to be able to act on her convictions would be even more difficult than it is.

If we turn again to the idea of developing virtues, not as an alternative to all other conceptions of values education but as, arguably, a richer conception that can take into account reason, feeling and emotion (Haydon 2003), then the importance of the ethical environment is all the more clear. Most theorists of virtue emphasise that if a person is to develop a certain virtue, as a settled disposition of character, then from an early age she has to be brought up in the right habits of action. This will only happen if others both instruct her and set a consistent example. For instance, a child is not likely initially to develop habits of acting fairly towards others unless her carers say to her things like 'it's not fair to take all of that for yourself: share it with your brother' *and* she experiences other people doing similar things. In other words, habits of evaluating behaviour in terms of fairness and of acting accordingly need to be present in the child's immediate environment if she is to develop such habits herself. If she does not develop such habits, then since (in a much-quoted remark of Aristotle) 'we become just by doing just acts' she will not have the basis for gradually developing a sense of fairness or justice as a settled character trait.

Not surprisingly, then, from Aristotle onwards it has been recognised that the primary condition for a person developing virtues has been that the person is brought up within an environment in which those virtues are recognised and practised. For Aristotle, the virtues to be developed were the virtues of citizens (exclusively male, and far fewer than the whole population) of Athens in the fourth century BC. He did not give much attention to the fact that different virtues might be developed in different times and places, though even in his own time the ranking of virtues would have been somewhat different in Athens and in Sparta. But it is now recognised (and has been especially stressed by MacIntyre (1981)) that one community can differ from another in the virtues that it prioritises and in the interpretation of virtues that ostensibly go by the same name. This raises issues that are very pertinent to societies in which a variety of ethical traditions interact. Some, including MacIntyre (1999), consider that an education into a genuinely shared heritage of virtues cannot take place in a modern diverse society, while others (Carr 2003; Katayama 2003) believe that there can be sufficient common ground.

This section has brought out two ways in which the ethical environment is important to values education. First, that values education is more likely to be successful in any individual case if the surrounding ethical environment is such that it lends support to what the educator is trying to do.[3] For young children, it will be their immediate local environment, beginning with family or household, that makes most difference. Once children are in school they are already susceptible to a wider range of environmental influences, and by the time they are adolescents in school they are capable of knowing as much as many adults know about the global ethical environment. Second, the content of formal values education is likely to vary from one society to another to the extent that the generally recognised values of the society vary (and this point holds whether we are thinking in terms of rules, principles or virtues). It is not impossible for schools to try to work counter to perceived tendencies in the wider society, but (given the first point) it will be harder to succeed in that task.

The ethical environment in the development of virtues

Accounts of values education that centre on the development of virtues raise some particular issues of their own that I shall consider in this section and the next. We have seen that in order to develop a virtue a person may need to be brought up to act in the right sort of way, even perhaps initially following rules. But when the virtue is fully developed, what is happening is no longer a following of rules. We know this partly because the virtuous person is able to make finer discriminations, be more responsive to the particular features of situations, than could be possible through following rules. But we also know (according to a common picture of virtues) that she is not going through some articulated process of reasoning. So what is going on?

It may help to consider our own experience, even if we would not claim any well-developed degree of virtue for ourselves. We need to think of occasions when we feel, 'intuitively' as we may say, what is the right thing to do, or that some course of action could not be the thing to do. There must be, in the jargon of the computer age, some processing of information going on (or our judgement would not be a response to the situation at all) but it is not, or need not be, happening consciously. To make sense of this we need to think of the perceptual element. We are perceiving, to a greater or lesser degree, more or less accurately, the ethically salient features of a situation. These are real features of a situation (they may include, for instance, the qualities displayed in other people's actions: this person is being tactful, that person is well-meaning but clumsy, and so on), but they are features that would not be perceived by a person, or animal, operating purely with the untutored perceptual capacities given by physiology. How do we come to be able to perceive such features? The answer has to be that we have been inducted into a way of perceiving, and that must be through being inducted into a way of life in which that way of seeing plays a part. Our sensibilities, such as they are, have developed within an ethical culture (Lovibond 2002). Exposure to this culture, then, is vital; sufficient exposure for a person to build up a stock of experience necessarily takes time. Some virtue theorists stress that vicarious experience, as in the thoughtful reading of literature (Smith 1997, 2003), can supplement personal experience. The processes will be similar, whatever the details of the local ethical environment. Had we been brought up in a different ethical environment, we might perceive other – but equally real – features as ethically salient.

If that is how the perceptual aspect of virtues develops, what of the motivational aspect? Here an initial upbringing within certain patterns of action will do much of the work, by getting a person accustomed to acting in certain ways, and if necessary to resisting immediate counter-inclinations. But a problem begins to appear in this kind of account. For a virtue-based account of values education to work we have to assume (what seems very plausible) that the developing person is sensitive, and susceptible, to influence from the ethical environment. But now we have to note also that virtues are, quite standardly among virtue theorists (again starting with Aristotle), considered to be rather stable dispositions of a person. They are often referred to as character traits, and we do not call something a trait of a person's character unless we think it is long lasting rather than ephemeral. (Stable character traits are not necessarily good, of course, but we will not call them virtues unless we do think they are good.) As Hursthouse puts it:

> One important fact about people's virtues and vices is that, once acquired, they are strongly entrenched, precisely because they involve so much more than mere tendencies to act in certain ways. A change

in such character traits is a profound change, one that goes 'all the way down'.

Hursthouse 1999: 12

If a character trait is strongly entrenched, that means that the person concerned will not be simply a follower of fashion, will not modify her judgements and her conduct because other people around her are changing theirs, will not, in short, be subject to fluctuations in the surrounding ethical climate. But notice Hursthouse's phrase 'once acquired'. It seems that while acquiring a virtue a person has to be susceptible to the ethical environment, or the virtue could not be acquired at all; once the virtue is acquired, then by definition the person is no longer (very) susceptible to the ethical environment, since her character trait will remain stable in the face of it. But this makes it sound as if there is some mysterious cut-off point, at which a person suddenly changes from being susceptible to not being susceptible to environmental influence.

That a virtue has to be acquired over a long period of susceptibility to an appropriate kind of environment seems to have psychological realism on its side (Flanagan 1991). This very fact should make us cautious about accepting the realism of the picture of a virtue as a thoroughly entrenched stable trait immune from environmental influences. In the next section we shall see grounds for this caution in the work of some social psychologists. For the moment, we need at least to recognise that having a virtue is a matter of degree (as Hursthouse goes on to acknowledge). Someone might, presumably, go on gradually acquiring a virtue for a long time, so that there might never be a point at which we could say 'she has (fully) acquired it'. And therefore we would never be able to say that there has come a point beyond which her conduct and her feelings and motivation are entirely the outcome of her own trait of character rather than responses to her environment. Besides, someone's environment is never all of a piece. The normal process of upbringing is one in which at first it is only what is immediate and local in a child's environment that is salient to her, while later a much larger and more diverse environment comes into view. So we can make sense of what seems to be the case, that if someone is brought up in a local environment that encourages them to question what they are told they may retain a tendency to question the features of the wider environment in which they later find themselves, while if they are brought up in an environment that encourages conformity they may be more likely to conform to whatever tendencies they find in their later environment.

We also, of course, have to recognise that some environments are much tougher ones for virtues to survive in than are others (and that for many of us whatever virtues we may have acquired or partially developed may have been relatively untested). The ethical environment of the Nazis was clearly one of the toughest. Hursthouse writes of it:

> One reason, I take it, that we judge the Nazis so severely is that, although it might well take a quite exceptional person to see through the anti-Semitism so well entrenched at that time (in the UK and US as well as in Germany and Austria), there was nothing entrenched about the idea that it would be just policy to start drawing distinctions between the legal rights of your country's citizens on grounds of race, let alone the idea that it was consistent with compassion and justice to put them in concentration camps and slaughter them. Anyone reasonably decent in Europe at the time, however anti-Semitic their upbringing, was able to see that it was wrong.
>
> Hursthouse 1999: 148–149

Assuming we agree with Hursthouse's conclusion here, we are still only saying something about the possibility of making a cognitive judgement that the Nazi policies were wrong (utterly wrong, evil). We have to think that the ordinary German of the time was capable of making that judgement. But to put such a judgement into practice, to stand up against the ethical environment of the time, would have needed a certain quality of character, the presence of virtues fully developed in more than just perceptual and cognitive aspects. The values education of the time, of course, would have been unlikely to produce in the younger generation the virtues that could stand up to the Nazi environment, since it was just that environment into which it was inducting people. But we may well wonder how far even the best education we can imagine now would be successful in producing character traits immune to that environment.

Virtues and situationist psychology

Is there something mistaken in the first place in the picture of a strongly entrenched character trait? We will often refer to assumed traits to explain why some people behave in one way in a given situation, other people in a different way. If, for instance, we want to explain why some students cheat in their coursework, we may think that some have not developed the character trait of honesty and others have. Many empirical studies[4] have suggested that situational factors – such as the presence or absence of the opportunity to cheat – are better predictors of whether people actually will cheat than any assumed underlying traits. It is worth recalling here the distinction made in

Chapter 1 between situation and environment. The relevant ethical environment will often be rather similar across different studies of cheating: an environment in which at least lip service is paid to the idea of honesty, and in which on the whole it is probably convenient and not too difficult for people to be honest in their daily lives, but in which striking examples of honesty upheld in the face of temptation and opportunity (the kinds of example Kant would have favoured) are rare.

The situationist approach in social psychology questions the extent to which individual behaviour, and especially the differences between the behaviour of one individual and of another, can be explained by individual dispositions such as character traits, or the presence or absence of virtues. There are certain classic studies to which reference is often made. One is Milgram's study of obedience to authority, already mentioned in Chapter 1. Another is an attempt to replicate experimentally the parable of the Good Samaritan, by Darley and Batson (1973). These researchers asked student priests to prepare a talk and then walk to a nearby building to present it. *En route* to give the talk, each student encountered a man lying in the way, clearly in some trouble. Some students stopped to help, others walked by. One can *try* to differentiate here, as Darley and Batson did, in terms of the character traits of different students; perhaps those who wanted to be priests for altruistic reasons could exemplify one kind of virtue, those who sought their own spiritual fulfilment, another. One can also speculate about the broader ethical environment within which the experiment takes place: there would have been certain ideas and attitudes that the students brought to the situation, and among those would be their own prior acquaintance with the parable of the Good Samaritan. But the only variable that could be shown to be significant in distinguishing the good Samaritans from the rest was a situational one that Darley and Batson built into the experiment: whether the student was or was not told that he was running late. Those in a hurry, regardless of the other variables, were less likely to stop.

In our everyday explanations of people's actions we often bring traits of character into the story. The Good Samaritan had the virtue of compassion; the Pharisee lacked that virtue but had the vice of hypocrisy. If one person does not steal it is because that person is honest; if another does it is because that person is dishonest. And so on. Situationist social psychology, building on experiments such as those mentioned, has questioned this assumption. The term *fundamental attribution error* has been coined for the error (if it is indeed an error) of thinking that there are stable character traits that account for the differences in people's conduct (Ross and Nesbitt 1991).

Since those classic studies there have been fewer studies that appear so dramatic in their results (no doubt in part because the deception of the experimental subjects that was an integral part of the studies by Milgram and by Darley and Batson would probably now be ruled out by a research ethics committee). But the overall idea of situationism is still very much alive. The recent focus has perhaps been not so much on what it is that actually explains why one individual behaves in one way and another in another way, but more on the *folk psychology* of the assumptions that people innocent of academic psychology tend to make about such explanations. The term *correspondence bias* has been used for people's widespread tendency to think that the explanation of people's behaviour (other people's and even their own) rests in personal qualities rather than in the external situation (Gilbert and Malone 1995). Empirical investigation of this bias continues; one of the most recent examples is a study, in the wake of the destruction of the Twin Towers in New York on 11 September 2001, of the variables in American subjects' tendencies to attribute terrorist actions to the motivations of individuals or to the situation in which they found themselves (Riggs and Gumbrecht 2005).

That people do have a bias towards explaining behaviour by reference to personal qualities rather than to the situation may well be a truth of folk psychology (subject, needless to say, to many qualifications). That there are actually no such things as stable personal qualities that can make a difference to how people behave would be a much stronger claim and far more difficult to establish. While the majority of philosophical writers on virtues have not taken the claims of situationist social psychology into account, those who have[5] have responded with varying degrees of caution about the psychological reality of virtues. Annas (2003) makes the important point that to reject the reality of virtues because of the demonstrable relevance of the situation in explaining behaviour is to misconstrue the nature of virtues. As has been said above, to have a virtue is not to have a settled pattern of behaviour that leads one blindly to act in a given way regardless of the surrounding situation. On the contrary, the virtuous person is one who does take the situation into account and responds to it in the appropriate way.

Whatever our conclusion on the reality and stability of virtues, we need to recognise the importance of situational and environmental factors. Situational factors may, outside the realms of experimental social psychology, be unpredictable and uncontrollable; at least we should not be over-sanguine that if only we could properly educate people they would be immune to such factors. The broader ethical environment is a different matter again. Not only is the quality of our ethical environment an important influence on how adults behave towards one another; it is also an important influence on the success or otherwise of whatever values education we attempt to undertake. It is possible that in one respect values education really was easier in a relatively homogeneous society like Aristotle's, just because there would have been greater consistency in the influences to which a young person was exposed. We must, however, remember the plurality of values. Consistency is not everything: we may have ample reason for favouring a diverse, tolerant but inconsistent environment over a homogeneous, oppressive and consistent one.

Whatever the truth may be about the reality of stable character traits, the idea of such traits, the language we use to name them, and our tendency to attribute them to people, are in themselves important parts of our ethical environment. The notion of a person who possesses certain virtues can function as a regulative idea for us. Any one of us could ask, 'What would a compassionate – or generous, or sensitive – person do in a case like this?' and we may find that we can answer such a question, not, of course, through any empirical investigation, but by working through our own understanding of what it is to be such a person. Then, too, we can use the language of virtues to evaluate actions as well as character traits (as in Aristotle's remark, 'we become just [persons] by doing just actions'). In using that language we may provide reasons for action to young people ('don't be cruel', 'this would be a kind thing to do') which may make a difference, even if the idea that they will thereby develop settled character traits should turn out to be an illusion.

The findings of situationist psychology, then, have not so far given us any strong reason to abandon using the language of virtues, perhaps especially when we wish to encourage people by praising them. On the other hand, we – especially when relating to children – should be wary of using the language of vices (settled *bad* character traits) in blaming people. If people sometimes live up to our positive expectations of them, they may also live down to our negative expectations. People who have acted dishonestly on occasion may be more likely to continue acting dishonestly if we have labelled them 'dishonest' as persons. The attribution error, to the extent that it really is an error, may turn our attention away from factors in the environment that we should be addressing.

The same might be said, with varying degrees of force, of all the conceptions of values education that we have surveyed in this chapter. Even if their starting point is a desire for the good of the whole society rather than for the individual good of each person being educated, these approaches to values education concentrate on the difference that education can make to individual behaviour or thought or dispositions. In doing that, they may pay too little attention to the ethical environment. Perhaps there is an implicit assumption that if the education of individuals proceeds in the right fashion, the ethical environment will come right of its own accord. But if we complement such approaches by a more explicit attention to the environment, other ways of thinking about values education come into view.

The remaining chapters of this book will suggest two ways of thinking about the tasks of education in relation to values. One takes the perspective of the flourishing of society: it sees education as one of the ways in which society can nurture and sustain the quality of its ethical environment. The other takes the perspective of the flourishing of the individual: it sees education as one of the ways in which people can be helped to find their way through (rather than simply being inducted into) the complexities of the ethical environment surrounding them. Part of my argument will be that these two perspectives on values education are compatible and complementary.

4 Taking responsibility for the ethical environment

The importance of the ethical environment should now be clear. What is less clear is whether there is anything we can do about the quality of our ethical environment. It is only quite recently that many of us have become used to thinking that we share a responsibility for the quality of our *physical* environment. Can we take responsibility for the quality of our *ethical* environment? And if we can, what will the implications be for education?

If we are to take responsibility for the quality of our ethical environment, several other things will have to be true of us and our thinking. I shall briefly list these points here (in an order that need not be taken chronologically), before beginning to explore them.

The first essential, then, is to recognise the existence of the ethical environment, to get away from the invisibility of its workings to which Blackburn (2001: 2) refers. And, of course, we must recognise its importance. Then, we have to recognise: that the ethical environment is not static, but can indeed change quite rapidly; that its changes are not matters of indifference to us, but that we can make some assessment of whether our ethical environment is changing for better or for worse; and that the changes do not just happen independently of us, but that we can consciously contribute to or try to resist the changes.

Then, we have to be sufficiently self-reflective to ask who is this 'we' that is to take responsibility? Is it to be each one of us individually? Or some group, or all of us, collectively? And if responsibility is to be taken collectively, through what practical processes can this be done? Until we get to that question, I shall take it that 'we' can embrace anyone and everyone.

In this chapter I shall address these points in turn. In doing so, I shall sometimes draw an analogy between our relationship to our physical environment and our relationship to our ethical environment. It is not that there is a point-by-point comparison between the two kinds of environment. The analogy concerns ourselves in both cases, and how we stand vis-à-vis these environments.

This chapter will have rather less to say, explicitly, about education than other chapters. Implicitly, it addresses educational concerns throughout, in two ways. First (and as relevant to non-teachers as to teachers) if we recognise the importance of education, and we recognise the relevance to education of the kind of ethical environment in which we live, then we must take seriously our responsibility for that environment. This holds whether we take 'education' as equivalent to schooling, or as being broader. Brighouse, after arguing for certain central goals of schooling, expresses his hope 'that non-teachers . . . will see themselves, and society as a whole, as responsible for creating an out-of-school environment for children that supports, rather than inhibits, schools in their pursuit of these goals' (Brighouse 2006: 135). It only needs to be added that, taking education now in a broader sense, we may see the ethical environment as potentially being educative directly, not only indirectly through the way it supports schools.

The considerations in this chapter are directly relevant to schools in a second way also. It cannot be only the readers of this book who share a responsibility for the quality of the ethical environment. We must hope that future generations will also take on that responsibility. So we need to educate them to do so. That means that the questions discussed in this chapter – how people can take responsibility for their ethical environment, how they can decide which changes are for the better, how they can try to bring about those changes – are questions that students in schools ought to be discussing. The issues considered in this chapter should, I submit, form part of the content of education for citizenship.

Attending to the ethical environment

Much of the time we take our ethical environment for granted, even while we live our lives within it. Of course, we have been inducted into it, we are constantly influenced by it, and we are drawing on its resources whenever we make any ethical evaluation, think about what to do, and so on. (Unlike some of the resources of the natural environment, those the ethical environment contains are not liable to run out, since they consist of ideas, vocabulary, opinions, and so on; but we shall see later that they could become attenuated in a different way.) To see how the workings of the ethical environment can be invisible we can make use of a philosophical distinction between first-order and second-order thinking. When we are thinking about what to do, or evaluating something, this is first-order thinking; when we reflect on that kind of thinking, wondering about *how* we decide what to do, what basis we have for our evaluations, and so on, we are entering into second-order thinking. Engaging in second-order thinking about our ethical environment is, for many people, not a common practice.

This is not to say that thinking about our ethical environment is a new phenomenon in the world. Philosophers have always thought about our ethical environment (albeit not using that terminology), often concentrating on some particular aspect of it (ideas of right and wrong, ideas of personal well-being, conceptions of justice, and so on). So, often, have theologians. In recent times psychologists, sociologists and anthropologists have made empirical studies of various aspects of the ethical environment. And journalists and other media commentators often write about the climate of opinion that they observe in society. But for many people, much of the time, even if they read such writing, there is not much occasion to stop and think about the ethical environment in which we move. It is possible that this is especially true in a secular society. Religious practices do sometimes call attention to the ethical environment. The point here is not simply that sermons, addresses, homilies and the like may contain moral exhortations – that is first-order discourse – but that thoughtful religious leaders will have something to say on second-order matters such as the relation between moral demands and aspirations to a spiritual life, or between moral laws and virtues. Many practising religious believers may be afforded the opportunity for reflection on their ethical environment at least once a week, and that may be more frequent than is true for many who are outside religious practices.

Meanwhile, schooling, which for so many children is almost a daily part of their experience for large parts of their lives, could do far more than it does to direct attention towards our ethical environment.

Changes in the ethical environment

When we do reflect on the ethical environment, one of the clearest points about it is its propensity to change. This has been implicit already throughout this book. The ethical environment of the Ik went through a major change after they were moved to a different territory. The ethical environment of the Nazis came into being within about a decade, and disappeared still more quickly, except that it is not quite right to say that it has disappeared. Something as traumatic as that does not disappear without trace; as we saw in Chapter 1, it has changed our ethical environment by the very fact that we are aware of what happened.

Traumatic examples remind us of how fragile the ethical environment, like the natural environment, can turn out to be. But we can observe less traumatic and more piecemeal changes around us during our own lives. To many people in the world, but perhaps most of all in Europe, an increasing liberalisation has been a significant change during their lifetimes. This may be most evident in attitudes towards personal and sexual relationships. What used to be widely seen as unacceptable or frowned upon (even if tolerated) has become acceptable or even normal. In England this has happened in the course of, say, three decades in relation to people of opposite sexes living together without marriage; it seems to be in the process of happening in relation to people of the same sex living in a sexual relationship. The point is not, of course, that there is any unanimity about this; we are talking about a prevailing climate of opinion. There have also been changes relating to the kind of language that is acceptable in public contexts – for instance in relation to women and to ethnic minorities. And attitudes on the acceptability of smoking and on the use of other drugs are changing. These are only some of the more obvious examples of change.

An attempt has been made here to outline these changes in a neutral language. Nothing said above implies that the changes have been improvements or have been deteriorations. You may think that some of these changes have been for the worse – that our ethical environment has been deteriorating in some of these respects. You may also think that there are certain unchanging ethical standards, which are in some sense *true* independently of any changing circumstances. The focus in this book on the ethical environment is intended to presuppose *neither* that there are *nor* that there are not unchanging ethical truths. It is important, not least for the practical business of education that cannot be suspended while we seek philosophical agreement, that we can focus on our ethical environment without having to engage in that kind of search for foundations (see the Introduction). But we need to take care in how we interpret the way that unchanging truths could relate to a changing ethical environment. Suppose there are unchanging ethical truths – unchanging because they are given by God, or laid up in heaven, or somehow, in a phrase philosophers sometimes use, built into the fabric of the world. Then in some way these truths must be capable of existing not as part of our ethical environment but outside it. If these truths really have their existence or their origin outside of human life, then it is conceivable that human beings might have failed to recognise them. They would not then exist as ideas within the ethical environment.[1] If the notion of an ethical truth existing entirely unrecognised seems too paradoxical, then consider that some ethical beliefs that by now have spread widely across the global ethical environment – the wrongness of slavery, for instance, or the moral equality of the sexes – have had very little salience within some former ethical environments. If there *are* unchanging ethical truths, they make a difference within the world only insofar as they are recognised by at least some people, that is, insofar as they have become part of the ethical environment.

Evaluating the ethical environment

When we evaluate an action as right or wrong, or a state of affairs as good or bad, or when we pick out qualities of a person for praise or denigration, we are making a move within our ethical environment, using the ideas it makes available to us; the first part of Chapter 2 reviewed many of the ways in which we can do this. But this raises a question: how can we evaluate our ethical environment itself? We cannot make an evaluation from any standpoint totally outside our ethical environment, because if we could step outside it we would have no basis on which to make any evaluation at all. We can ignore our ethical environment for certain purposes, for instance while doing certain kinds of science, even, arguably (but controversially) the sort of social science that can describe our ethical environment and the changes in it. But if we want to assess whether those changes are for better or for worse we have to work from within the ethical environment again.

Such a situation is not unfamiliar to modern philosophy; there is even a word for it: Neurathian (cf. Hursthouse 1999: 166). The Austrian theorist Otto Neurath used the metaphor of a boat that has to be repaired while at sea, with no possibility of bringing it into a dry dock. It is impossible to take it to pieces all at once and rebuild it. But, so long as enough of it is afloat to provide a platform on which to stand, other parts can be repaired and improved. Some philosophers have applied the metaphor to the whole conceptual scheme that a community of speakers uses. If we ask whether our conceptual scheme is the best available, we can only look at it from inside; but because we can notice a lack of fit between one part of that scheme and another, or see that some parts are less indispensable than others, we can revise it from within.

In the case of our ethical environment, given that it is very diverse, it is possible to use one part of it as a standpoint from which we can evaluate some other part. Sometimes we make a judgement on the whole of what we see as an all-embracing ethical environment. This is what is happening when we condemn the Nazi environment. Though we do this from outside that particular environment, we have no lack of standpoints within our own from which to evaluate it. If we can evaluate a whole ethical environment that we know exists or has existed, then we can in principle evaluate an ethical environment which we can imagine existing in the future – and this may be a direct descendant of the one in which we are now living, perhaps after tendencies that we now recognise have worked themselves out further. (The standards we might appeal to in evaluating an ethical environment will be the topic of a later section (p. 87).)

There is a certain artificiality in evaluating what we may take to be 'a whole ethical environment', since no local ethical environment – today at any rate – exists in complete isolation from what is around it. A more commonplace experience is that by taking into account some aspects of our own ethical environment we find ourselves unhappy with other aspects of it. So, for instance, someone who is not averse to the values that go with a culture of consumerism and materialism – including enjoyment, comfort, appreciation of good design – may also be aware that there are possibilities of finding meaning and value in life from something else besides working and consuming, and so may be unhappy with their own ethical environment even while caught up in it. In a similar way, looking to the future, we may consider, from a standpoint within our current ethical environment, whether we think certain changes would be for the better or for the worse. But we also have to recognise that the changing of the ethical environment *is* in part a changing of the prevailing standards by which evaluations of that very environment are made. That is what happens with the kind of change in the political environment of education to which Ball (2003) and others have referred; ways of acting that previously would not have occurred to people come to be seen as options; what once would have been widely recognised as unacceptable comes to be seen as normal, as what everyone does. It comes to be taken for granted, for instance, that part of the purpose of any school principal should be to enhance the standing of his or her school in the league tables; it comes to be seen as normal that the selection of students for entry to particular examinations will be carried out partly with the school's standing in the league tables in mind.

Yet the fact that prevailing standards change does not remove the possibility of criticising the standards (the very existence of the criticism shows that). Ways of thinking that were prevalent at an earlier time can be remembered or recovered from history. And those who believe that there are unchanging ethical truths, and that they know what those truths are, will have those truths (as they take them to be) available to them as standards by which to evaluate the changing environment. This does not affect the point made above that all evaluations are made from within the ethical environment; the very recognition of such standards brings them within that environment, even if they are salient only to a minority of people. This is one respect in which, as will be argued further below, we can evaluate internal diversity in the ethical environment as good; without diversity, the prevailing values may come to be the only ones recognised.

Changing the ethical environment

An earlier subheading was 'changes in the ethical environment' (p. 75). The current subheading '*changing* the ethical environment', draws attention to our being actively involved in the changes, rather than passively experiencing them. To recognise that the ethical environment does change is not yet to say that we can consciously and deliberately change it. And to think it is improving or deteriorating is not yet to say that we can do anything about enhancing or reversing such changes. Until quite recently, when people saw changes going on within the physical environment around them, they were liable to think that there was nothing they could do about these changes even if they were for the worse. Now we realise the extent to which we have brought about changes in the physical environment in the past through our own human activity. We also recognise that our activity will continue to have effects on the environment in the future, and that through the decisions we make we can to some degree alter the quality and extent of those effects.

Are we in a parallel situation in our relationship to the ethical environment? There is a difference, of course, in that changes in the physical environment are themselves physical changes. Changes in our ethical environment are changes within a world of ideas. But we should not exaggerate the difference. We are constantly taking action that brings about changes in a world of ideas: that, after all, is what we do in education. By educating one generation we pass on ideas, knowledge, ways of thinking; changing the details of our engagement in education may change what it is that we pass on, making a difference to the way that the next generation thinks. Nor is there any special difficulty in the fact that, from within our current ethical environment, we can think about changes in that very environment. This need be no more mysterious that the fact that, using our current language, we can reflect on this language and introduce neologisms and new metaphors into it, or decide that some terms are better avoided.

So, can we change our own ethical environment? In some sense it must be that changes in our ethical environment come about through human agency; although, as noted in Chapter 1, changes in the physical environment can have a causal influence on the ethical environment, this can happen only through the effects of the physical environment on humans. There are no purely physical processes that can themselves constitute changes in the ethical environment. Changes in what people find acceptable or unacceptable, in the standards that people use, in what some people blame others for, and so on, are changes in human thinking and activity ('activity' because blaming, criticising, praising and so on are things we *do* in a public world, not private thought processes). The important question is how far we can consciously and deliberately bring about the changes.

We might start by considering how much any one individual might do. Not much, we probably think. On the other hand, it is not difficult to recall certain particular individuals who have changed the ethical environment of their own day and sometimes that of many generations since. The prophets, founders and leaders of the major world religions are the most striking examples. In more recent times some political activists have surely had a significant effect on currents of ethical thinking: Mahatma Gandhi, Martin Luther King and Nelson Mandela are among the most obvious examples. Intellectuals have perhaps generally had somewhat less influence in changing the course of people's thinking about what is right and wrong or good and bad, but one would certainly have to include Marx and Darwin among important influences.

Individuals, then, can make a difference. We might still think that, in contrast to certain people whose influence has been exceptional, the average 'ordinary' individual can do nothing to effect the ethical environment. This need not be so. While we may think we can distinguish exceptional from ordinary individuals, any difference in their personal qualities must be one of degree; and besides, if we recall the discussion in the last chapter, we must recognise that an individual's exceptional influence may owe much to their exceptional situation.

Virtually no one goes through life without making some difference to somebody, and we can rarely be certain what the effects of our words and actions may be (that is one of the difficulties within utilitarian thinking). An example set, a casual piece of praise or blame, a decision to tolerate or not to tolerate another's actions, a comment that some issue is a moral issue, not a purely practical one, can influence another, who will influence others in turn, and so on. To say this is *not* to subscribe to *methodological individualism*, the position within the philosophy of the social sciences which holds that all facts about human society (which must include the nature of the ethical environment and changes within it) can ultimately be reduced to the thoughts and actions of individuals. The surrounding environment of ideas and values is real enough, and it has already influenced each of us when we are influencing others. Besides, it is not difficult to think of changes in the ethical environment that cannot be explained purely as the cumulative effect of the decisions of many individuals.

Just one example may suffice for the moment: changes in the acceptability of overt expressions of racism, even at what may appear to be the personal level of an individual's use of language. Racist language may be used less than it used to be, and may be more likely to meet with the disapproval of others when it is used. How do we explain such changes (to whatever extent they have actually happened, which may be different in different countries)? If we were to say that many people have, in this particular respect, become more moral, that would be no explanation. Even if we believe in the underlying reality of virtues, it would be quite implausible to say that thousands or millions of individuals, spontaneously and coincidentally, have become more virtuous. In fact at an individual level more than one kind of change may be happening. Some people may be consciously refraining from using such language, without necessarily any underlying change in attitude; other people may have undergone a change in attitude so that it no longer occurs to them to use such language. But in many, probably most, cases such changes in individuals will not be the result either of their own unprompted reflection or of some kind of conversion experience.

One explanatory factor in many cases is legislation, quite deliberately introduced in order to effect changes in behaviour. Legislation that outlaws certain forms of action (which may include action carried out through speech, such as incitement to racial hatred) does not have its effect only by setting up concrete disincentives to certain forms of behaviour. It can also have an effect through its influence on public attitudes. The mere fact that something has been made an object of legislation can draw explicit attention to it, and the fact that something is illegal will for many people invest it with a certain negative aura (it will not necessarily have this effect for all, since some people may rebel against legal restrictions).

Another explanatory factor is, not surprisingly, formal education. Schools may do their best to eliminate racist language, and they may have a number of reasons for doing so. In part, the aim may be directly to protect those students and staff who might be the victims of racist language. Another aim is to influence the underlying attitudes of those inclined to use such language, on the grounds that it is better for people (even apart from consideration for the potential victims) if they are free from prejudice. Both aims are most likely to succeed if a school can create an ethos that is positively supportive of friendly and respectful relations between people of different ethnic groups, rather than merely targeting the behaviour it wants to eliminate.

There is also the hope, of course, that people whose education has taken place in such an ethos will go on to contribute to an ethical environment that mirrors that ethos in the wider society. One would have to be very sceptical about the effects, both of bringing together in schools children of different ethnic backgrounds, and of deliberate anti-racist policies and practices, to think that these have not contributed something to the changes in public attitudes.

There are, of course, many other factors which also contribute to such changes. Mass media are undeniably influential. Within liberal societies two facts about the media are clearly important: that they are to a large extent not under government control, and that (partly as a result of that) they can send very mixed messages. Anyone is likely, from their own perspective, to find some of the influence of the media negative rather than positive. But there is at least the possibility, within an uncontrolled media, that against whatever is negative there will be some counterinfluence. What is more difficult to assess is the extent to which public opinion is formed by the media. Certainly for most of us, what we take to be our *knowledge* of public opinion comes largely through the media; it is less clear how far what *constitutes* public opinion is formed by media reporting. In any case, formal education needs to take into account and alert people to the power of mass media.

It may be that governmental influence should give more cause for concern because it can be less overt and its consequences rather unpredictable; some of the ethical issues arising from deliberate governmental intervention in the ethical environment will be discussed in the next chapter. Not all ethical changes resulting from government action will be deliberate. It is perhaps a moot point how far market-oriented policies, not least within schooling, have been *intended* to bring about some change in the ethical environment, such as a decreasing trust in professionals on the part of the general public. Presumably at least some reported changes have not been intended; an example would be the willingness of some headteachers to 'fiddle the figures' (because everyone does it) as mentioned in Chapter 1. Many commentators would agree that, whether intended or not, such changes constitute a significant shift in the ethical environment in which older notions of professional responsibility and professional judgement, exercised directly in relation to the relevant public, are being displaced by the idea of accountability towards government (Bottery 2004: 102; Green 2004).

To change or not to change?

The upshot so far is that we *can* make a difference to our ethical environment. In part, we make this difference through what we do and say, without aiming to make any such difference. But we could also consciously have such an aim.

What, more precisely, might that aim be? A starting assumption would be that we will want changes in our ethical environment to be improvements rather than deteriorations. Logically, it is not to be taken for granted that there is room for improvement. Perhaps the ethical environment in which we now live is the best that it could be, so that any change must be a deterioration; but once stated that seems an implausible speculation. There are too many examples ready to hand of human inhumanity to other humans, not to mention too many cases of people doing nothing to improve the lot of others when they could be doing something. Any change in the surrounding climate of ideas that would have a restraining influence on cruelty, or that would be conducive to more positive beneficence, would surely be an improvement. But there is a rather different thought that may have more force. Those who are worried by this thought might express it as follows: our ethical environment has whatever power it does have just insofar as we do *not* think it is open to conscious manipulation. Once we think that it is open to us to change it, then it will cease to have that power, and it will then be easier to ignore it. So any change, even one that appears to be for the better, carries a greater danger with it.

We need to be careful in interpreting this worry. If we see certain aspects of our ethical environment as having an objective validity independently of our own thinking, then we are right to be cautious about any change that would be liable to undermine the *perceived* validity of these aspects. If, for instance, it is an objective truth that cruelty is wrong, then an ethical environment that encourages people to think that they can decide for themselves whether cruelty is wrong could lead to fewer people recognising that objective truth. To that extent, a change towards such an ethical environment would be a change for the worse. But this is far from being a strong argument for resisting *any* change in our ethical environment. A change that led towards fewer people engaging in cruelty would, by the standards set by that same objective truth, be a change for the better. The most important aspect of the change could be, not whether people do or do not believe that it is an objective truth that cruelty is wrong, but whether people are or are not *disposed* to be cruel, for whatever reason. (Whether people do or do not engage in cruelty may have rather little to do with their beliefs about any objective truths; for many people, it will have more to do with their underlying affective dispositions, and for some it may have a lot to do with what other people will think or with the example they see in the behaviour of others.)

One aspect of the present concern that we shall have to come back to is whether it is, by and large, dangerous for people to pay attention to and *think* about their own ethical environment. *If* that is dangerous, then much that will be said about values education in the rest of this book will be based on a false premise. More will be said on this in the next chapter, where the ideas of autonomy, indoctrination and manipulation will be discussed. In brief, the argument there will be that there need be nothing wrong with manipulating the ethical environment, so long as it can be done without manipulating people.

For the moment, we have a provisional basis on which to formulate what a reasonable aim could be in relation to our own ethical environment, given that its quality is not entirely outside our own control. We should not seek to preserve our ethical environment exactly as it is. That would be a reasonable aim only if we thought either that this environment is already perfect or that the dangers of any change at all outweigh the possibilities of change for the better. If we recognise, not only that improvement is theoretically possible, but that there are plausible instances of an improvement having actually come about (as perhaps in the reduction of discriminatory attitudes already mentioned), then our own relationship towards our ethical environment should be one that allows the possibility of change for the better. Here again we may be able to borrow from our thinking about our responsibility for the natural environment. In that case, we do not think that our aim should be to preserve the natural environment exactly as it now is; if we did that, we would be preserving the damage we have already done to it, and ruling out the possibility of reversing some of that damage. Ecologists speak of 'conserving' rather than 'preserving', and conserving does not rule out active intervention, where that intervention is the strategy most likely in the long term to limit deterioration. The same point is illustrated by conservation in the world of art, where preventing damage may require a degree of restoration.

For those who think that our ethical environment has already shown an overall decline compared with what it once was, restoration might seem the right idea. For those who take a more optimistic view, the idea of conserving the ethical environment – maintaining what is centrally important, while allowing for change in response to changing circumstances – may be more appropriate. Even 'conserving' may carry too much suggestion of a static condition. Still borrowing from the discourse of responsibility for the natural environment, it may be preferable to speak of 'sustaining' our ethical environment. But unpacking the connotations of that term will need to wait until we discuss further what the standards are by which we might assess the quality of our ethical environment.

At this point we have seen that several conditions are in place to support the thought that our relationship towards our ethical environment should be one, not of passive acceptance, but of active responsibility. It is possible for us to make a difference to our ethical environment, for better or for worse, and it is possible to evaluate this 'better' or 'worse'. It might seem that the next step in the argument would be to set out some criteria for making that assessment of better or worse. But for all that has been said so far, every individual might have their own idea as to what these criteria should be, according to their own preferences or their own first order moral beliefs. One person may, for instance, think that a desirable ethical environment is one in which there is widespread agreement on a certain set of ideas and very little controversy. Another may feel that it is more stimulating to live in an environment in which little is taken for granted and everything can be challenged. So far, however, these might be just individual preferences. If a person puts great store by her first-order belief that abortion equates to murder, she may be inclined to favour any kind of ethical environment (however oppressive it may appear to others) that reduces the incidence of abortion; while one who wants freedom of choice in that respect might hope to obtain it through an environment that favours freedom of individual choice generally, regardless of more specific considerations about the value of free choice in this or that respect.

If a particular ethical environment were to be judged purely by whether it tended to satisfy particular first-order convictions, no agreed criteria for the quality of the ethical environment would be possible. Discussions about the quality of the ethical environment might be, as perhaps too many discussions of ethical issues in the classroom are likely to be, no more than a trading of personal opinions. What is needed instead is an argument for broader, second-order standards that say something about the nature of the ethical environment overall. To see how such an argument is possible, we need to proceed by first answering a question we have so far deferred: who are the *we* who can take responsibility for our ethical environment?

Responsibility for the ethical environment

To return to the analogy with our relationship to the physical environment, we realise now (at least much more than we used to) the extent to which we are responsible for changes in our physical environment, in two senses of the term 'responsible'. First, we are causally responsible for many of the changes that take place; we brought about these changes through our human activities, and our activities will continue to have consequences for the environment in the future. Second, we are morally responsible. Possibly we blame ourselves for the deterioration that we have already caused; certainly we can recognise, as a matter of ethical thinking, that we *should* be more careful in the future, perhaps that we will be letting down future generations if we do not look after our environment, perhaps that we have a moral obligation to protect the environment. Thoughts of this latter kind are, of course, themselves moves that we make within our *ethical* environment.

What of that ethical environment itself, however? We can recognise our responsibility for it in the same ways. Human activities of many kinds – including conversation, writing, preaching, and legislation – have had a causal effect on our ethical environment.[2] We can recognise, then, that we can also have an effect on it in the future; and to that extent we can accept a moral responsibility for the quality of our ethical environment in the future.

Where exactly does the responsibility lie? In the case of the physical environment, there is no single locus of responsibility. We can each of us do something towards maintaining the quality of the physical environment through such actions as collecting bottles and newspapers for recycling and being more efficient in our use of energy. But we are aware that there are some things that can only be done effectively, or at all, through concerted action on a larger scale. Individual collecting of bottles and newspapers will not be effective if there are no facilities for recycling them, and those facilities will not necessarily be provided by private enterprise without government intervention. A switch on a large scale from private to public transport needs good public transport facilities to be provided, which again is unlikely to happen without deliberate government policy. The position is similar for increased use of renewable sources of energy. Government intervention can, of course, take many forms; it may not be direct government provision or funding but may include tax incentives and disincentives, as well as public education campaigns. And the level of government in question may be local or national and may in some cases need to involve intergovernmental cooperation.

The suggestion here is that responsibility for our ethical environment is similarly distributed. We can each in many small ways make a difference to our ethical environment, but there are some forms of action on the ethical environment that can only be undertaken collectively. Of the latter, some can be pursued through communities and voluntary organisations of many kinds, while some will require action at the level of government. One case in point already mentioned is the effect on the ethical environment of legislation on discrimination. Many other legislative examples could be cited. Health and safety legislation, for instance, often leads gradually to a change in public attitudes. Where initially there is a perceived interference in individual liberty (as with laws restricting smoking in public places), attitudes can change to the point where what previously was seen as a matter of personal choice is perceived as irresponsible and selfish, independently of the fact that it is illegal.

In modern states government exercises some degree of control over and responsibility for schooling. Individual parents, of course, will often be most concerned to achieve the best provision they can for their own children. But it is possible for parents also to be concerned about the quality of the schooling that is available to all in their society. Within a democratic political system, they have the possibility of having some influence on the quality of the schooling received, not only by their own children, but by all. If they support one party or another because of its educational policy, and do not have in mind *only* the difference the policy makes to their own children, then they are, as citizens, taking a degree of responsibility for the education received by all young people in their society.

If schooling is one of the major influences on the ethical environment, then it is one of the major channels through which individuals can take a degree of responsibility for their ethical environment. Parents can, of course, exercise this responsibility partly through the education they give their own children – especially if they are concerned with their children's development as ethical beings not only for the children's own sake but also for the sake of others. But all citizens can take a degree of responsibility for the ethical environment by seeking to influence the educational policy of government – provided the political system is sufficiently democratic.

The next chapter will look further into the ways in which government can seek to influence the ethical environment. We shall ask there whether educational channels of influence can reasonably be objected to on grounds of indoctrination or manipulation. For the moment, we can return to the issue of the standards by which the quality of the ethical environment might be judged. As indicated at the end of the previous section, the kind of standard we need is not one simply of consistency with this or that first-order moral belief. No ethical environment could be equally hospitable or equally supportive of all first-order beliefs. In the case of political institutions, it is at least arguable (and has often been argued by liberal theorists) that such institutions should display a kind of neutrality between different first-order commitments. In the case of the ethical environment as a whole, it would make no sense to demand neutrality. No doubt any existing ethical environment in any part of the world is biased in more or less subtle ways towards some points of view and against others; and the same would be true of any conceivable ethical environment. Anybody on the basis of their first-order views would find some ethical environments more congenial ones in which to live than others. But if all of us have some responsibility for the ethical environment that we have to share with others, there is an onus on us to do more than try to promote our own first-order views. We need to think about standards of evaluation that could reasonably be accepted – even if not whole-heartedly endorsed – within a system in which all could share in the responsibility for the quality of their ethical environment.

Standards for evaluating the ethical environment

First, then, we can suggest that an ethical environment may be a healthy or an unhealthy one for the people affected by it. We know roughly what it is for a physical environment to be unhealthy for people: some polluted environments, for instance, are directly conducive to certain diseases. Where this is the case, we can ask whether there is in the background a climate of ideas that allows the unhealthy physical environment to persist. Think, for instance, of cities at a stage of rapid industrialisation and correspondingly rapid growth in the population of unskilled and semi-skilled workers (perhaps in the early nineteenth century in parts of Britain and rather later in some other countries); the atmosphere and water supplies are polluted; water and air-borne diseases proliferate; there is extensive child labour; life expectancy is short. The ethical environment that tolerates this is itself a contributory factor to the ill health; changes in the surrounding climate of opinion can stimulate people to work for a gradual improvement in the physical environment.

An ethical environment, then, can sometimes be interpreted as contributing indirectly to physical health or ill health. More directly, an ethical environment may be psychologically unhealthy (though in saying this we have to recognise the contestability of any particular interpretation of psychological health; this notion itself lies inside our ethical environment). There is a kind of criticism that, especially perhaps since Freud, has been directed at ethical environments that are perceived as heavily moralistic, dominated by prohibitions that are difficult to observe and liable to induce guilt when they are broken. Such environments, especially if it is hard to see their bringing good consequences to anyone, may well appear on balance to be unhealthy ones (White 1990: Ch. 3; Rustin 1997).

It would be a mistake to think it is only heavily moralistic climates that might be conducive to psychological distress. In many Western countries today there is much greater acceptance of a wide variety of lifestyles, and with that goes a positive valuing of choice in almost every department of life; but a case can be made that this very valuing of choice does not bring happiness but imposes psychological burdens (Schwartz 2004). Even the awareness that other people are living by different standards could be a cause of distress to some, so that the idea of an environment that facilitates diversity of standards will by no means be welcome to all. Nevertheless, education has to prepare people at least to live with, if not to identify with, the kind of ethical environment they find around them for the moment.

There are also the difficulties that an ethical environment can impose on individuals who have to integrate conflicting demands into a single life, as mentioned in Chapter 2. The climate created by market-oriented and target-driven educational policies provides examples. Teachers have to 'play the game' of going along with the external demands, but many of them also have their own values, their own sense of what is important in education, and consider these values are not being well served by the external demands. For some, as noted at the end of Chapter 1, the result is demoralisation, a sense of guilt or loss of self-respect because teachers are not able to uphold the values that brought them into the profession in the first place. The ethical environment that exacts this cost is not a healthy one.[3]

The evaluation of an ethical environment as healthy or unhealthy draws on a weighing-up of consequences that is itself one of the evaluative moves our environment encourages us to take. Equally clearly, within any existing ethical environment, consequences are not everything. The assessment of some condition or state of affairs as healthy or unhealthy seems to call for the impartial view of an expert observer; but the perspective of individuals themselves must also count. The standard of health needs to be supplemented by a direct standard of inclusiveness, where that is taken to mean, not (impossibly) that all first-order views are equally realised, but that all *persons* can recognise themselves as sharing in the ethical environment.

We can ask whether all could see themselves, after reflection on their ethical environment, as having something invested in it – as being, in effect (to use a contemporary piece of political jargon) 'stakeholders' in the ethical environment. There may be those who have strong self-interested preferences that they wish to pursue, and who consequently experience the surrounding ethical environment primarily as putting constraints on them. Even they will gain a degree of protection of their interests from the fact that others live within the same ethical environment. The point of the idea of inclusiveness, however, is not that the consequences of the operation of the ethical environment should be beneficial, on balance, to every individual, whatever their own preferences; nor, as noted above, is the point that it should be possible for all first-order views to be put into practice.

The standard of inclusiveness makes an anti-discriminatory point: that a good ethical environment is such that no persons will be excluded from its benefits because of who they are. Thus the ethical environment of Nazi Germany in the years before the Holocaust was a bad one, not because Jews, disabled people and Romanies gained nothing at all from it, or because they lost far more than they gained from it, but because, given some of the major strands of thought within that very environment, they could not see themselves, and could not reasonably be expected to see themselves, as sharing in it on an equal footing with others; they could not in any sense identify with it or feel that they belonged to it. At bottom this is not a utilitarian point about consequences, but a more Kantian point about respect for the person. It leads to the recognition that any society that shares an ethical environment needs to have common elements within that environment, amounting to a sharing at least of some standards of morality in the narrow sense. And where once it might have seemed sufficient that such standards be shared within each nation, a global ethical environment demands that *some* standards be shared globally. The most obvious candidates are conceptions of human rights, which we shall touch on again below.

There is still more that we can add to a list of standards for the evaluation of the ethical environment. One point is that the environment should not, over time, be too fragile. Borrowing again from discourse about the natural environment, we can suggest that the ethical environment needs a degree of sustainability. Of course, where an ethical environment is thoroughly bad, we will be glad that it collapses; if the Nazi environment had proved to be sustainable for longer in the face of internal and external pressures that would have been bad, not good. So sustainability is certainly not in itself a criterion of a good ethical environment. But insofar as we think an existing ethical environment is worth having, even if it is far from perfect, we can reasonably hope that it will be sufficiently robust to accommodate some internal change without a collapse into chaos. As suggested above when the idea of 'conserving' the ethical environment was considered, it is important that the environment should not be inflexible, so that it can respond to changing circumstances while not losing what is most central and important. An ethical environment that can do this has the merit of sustainability.

The sustainability of an ethical environment over time is probably not causally independent of the extent to which it meets the standards of healthiness and inclusiveness. Slave-owning regimes, and the Nazi regime, were clearly not inclusive environments, and they were unhealthy environments, not only for their obvious victims, but arguably even for those who apparently benefited from them in the short term. Plausibly, their unhealthiness and exclusivity contributed to their downfall; but this falls far short of a demonstration that an unhealthy and exclusive environment could not survive. If we want a sustainable ethical environment we may be well advised to aim for an environment that can be healthy for all concerned and that all concerned can feel they are part of; but we should aim for those factors in any case.

The importance of diversity in the ethical environment

There is still one more putative standard for the quality of the ethical environment for which we might borrow a term from our discourse relating to the natural environment. This is the desirability of diversity, understood in a way that is compatible with some standards being shared. In the case of the natural environment there is a variety of reasons for favouring diversity, whether of landscapes, of habitats or of species. Some of these reasons may be aesthetic rather than ethical; we may simply think that a world containing many different sorts of landscape and habitat is a more beautiful world that any world that is all the same. We are familiar with the possibility of a somewhat similar preference regarding certain sorts of cultural diversity: we can think that diversity is good, a feature of the human world to be celebrated. At least, many people find no difficulty in that when the cultural products in question are to do with, say, food or the arts. A world in which there are many different kinds of food and many different traditions in music is much more interesting and richer than a monocultural world.

When we turn from what are primarily aesthetic values to ethical ones, it would be a mistake to overlook the greater complexity of the issues. It is not so clear that we should actively celebrate the fact that different people have very different views about how to live, especially since views about how to live include views about how to treat others. We cannot celebrate the existence of the Nazis, however determined we are to learn from the episode. Their morality is to be ruled out, in part at least because it is one that so many people could in no way have shared. But we should not forget that to many people this would seem too weak a reason for ruling it out. For people who believe in objective ethical truths, the position is not that certain norms are to be considered wrong because many people could not possibly accept them; rather it is that the norms are unacceptable, *ought* not to be accepted, because they are wrong. For believers in objective ethical truths, of whom there are many within liberal societies as in others, there may well be reasons for tolerating a diversity in values but there will be objective limits on the extent to which diversity can be positively valued, since the existence of values that are believed to be objectively wrong cannot be welcomed.

Nevertheless, there is an aspect of diversity that, it can be argued, should be welcome to believers in objective ethical truths as well as to sceptics about ethical objectivity. To see this we need to put the emphasis, not on diversity in the content of people's beliefs about what is right and what is wrong, but on the diversity to which we drew attention in Chapter 2: diversity in the kinds of element that go to make up a rich ethical environment.

Against a one-dimensional ethical environment

Again, without expecting an exact analogy, we may be able to borrow from discourse about the natural environment. Some of the reasons for seeking to retain biodiversity in nature have nothing to do with aesthetics. We know that the reduction of the gene pool and the reduction of the range of different habitats in the world can make the whole natural environment less adaptable to future changes which we cannot predict in detail. In the case of the ethical environment, the analogy is that we cannot know in detail what ethical challenges we may be faced with in future; we need a richness of ethical resources from which to respond.

Recall in the case of individuals the problem with reliance on rules about what is right and what is wrong. There can be no guarantee in advance that any set of such rules will be able to provide answers to all the issues that individuals may face in their lives. Rules, then, however valuable, cannot be a substitute for individuals being able to do their own thinking. Something similar applies to us collectively if we try to rely on too narrow a set of ethical ideas. Our contemporary problems in relation to the natural environment provide an illustration. Many modern societies relied for too long on an essentially instrumental idea that natural resources are available for human purposes without ethical restriction; now that unrestricted exploitation of these resources has led us into problems, we are still tempted to think primarily in instrumental and technical terms about what our response should be. At the same time we are increasingly recognising that the resources of morality in the narrow sense are hard to apply to our relationship with the natural environment (since notions of duty, obligation and rights are essentially notions formed within a world of human-to-human relationships). But there are other ways of thinking about the human relationship to the natural environment (Clark 1993; Cooper and Palmer 1998). Views that see human beings as a dependent part of the whole environment, rather than superior beings that can exploit it, have always been available within human cultures, but were largely sidelined for centuries in the developing West. We may be fortunate that ways of thinking about the natural environment which lie outside of morality in the narrow sense, and perhaps in current schemes of classification count as being aesthetic or spiritual, have never disappeared entirely from our ethical environment.

The point to be made here about diversity of ethical resources is not that all first-order views are equally to be welcomed, though even on that level we should keep in mind John Stuart Mill's (1975) point that any one view may ossify if it is never subject to debate. If the local climate of opinion is firmly set, say, against capital punishment, it may be that the existence of some individual voices on the opposite side is good for the vitality of that climate. But the point now being made about diversity is not so much about differences of opinion within the terms of one debate, but about the desirability of different *kinds* of ethical resources being readily available within the surrounding environment. We should be wary of our ethical environment coming to be one-dimensional.

What would be examples of a one-dimensional environment? Suppose our ethical discourse were purely utilitarian, in a rather narrow understanding of that way of thinking. Many philosophers who have advocated utilitarianism as an ethical theory, from Mill onwards, have been sensitive to a wide range of ethical considerations. Mill could very well say that we should seek to cultivate virtues and aesthetic sensibilities and imagination in ourselves and in our children, since in that way ultimately (human nature being what it is) there was more happiness to be found. But what is sometimes associated with utilitarianism, especially in political contexts, is a reductive way of thinking that, while focusing quite rightly on the consequences of policies for all concerned, seeks to assess all consequences against one standard measure. Often, the measure that comes most readily to hand is an economic one. In effect, everything is to be decided by cost–benefit analysis. This can lead to a dominance of instrumental thinking that can affect many areas of life, including education. It is not only that government policy will be of an instrumental kind, looking for good value for money in the results that schools produce, and that this will make it difficult for teachers not to think instrumentally themselves as they seek to meet government targets. More seriously perhaps, if the general ethos of the system is instrumental, it will tend to encourage rather than counteract instrumental thinking among the people being educated. Young people may be more likely to see their own lives in instrumental terms, where material well-being is what matters most and everything else in life is valued or not for what it contributes to that. The point here is not that this would be a wrong way of seeing one's life; rather that since there are other ways, an ethical environment that makes this way the default position is to that extent the poorer.

One possible antidote to an emphasis on instrumental calculation might be the view that ethical life has to be rooted in interpersonal *caring*. In Chapter 2 we noted the distinction claimed between the ethical orientations of caring and of justice. The writers who first propounded an ethics of care (Gilligan 1982; Noddings 1984) did so in a spirit of resistance to the one-dimensional emphasis that seemed to be present in much thinking of the time about moral development and moral education. But an ethic of caring would also be inadequate if it were all we had. A caring response can be contingent and seemingly arbitrary. At the end of 2004 there was an enormous and worldwide charitable response to the Indian Ocean tsunami disaster; nine months later the response to the earthquake in Pakistan and northern India seemed meagre in comparison. 'Compassion fatigue' may explain the lesser response, but leaves it open to criticism by standards of justice.

Before the advent in modern philosophical ethics of an ethic of care and of virtue ethics, it was Kantian ethics, as noted in Chapter 3, that was often held up in opposition to utilitarianism. It seeks to focus, not on consequences, but on human dignity. Would that not rescue us from the excesses, or at least the misinterpretations, of consequentialism? Perhaps, but Kant's moral compass, unlike real compasses, is better at telling people where not to go than at giving them a direction to follow. It will rule out ways of acting that are fundamentally disrespectful to others, but will leave largely open the question of what positively constitutes a good life. That is, of course, one of the reasons why Kant's ethics has been influential within a liberal tradition. But while it is a clear demand of liberal politics that the state should not tell people how to live their lives so long as they respect others, individuals themselves need something more to go on in their own decisions. More than Kant's ethics is needed in the ethical environment. Besides, Kantian ethics, being concerned with relationships between rational moral agents, has difficulty in saying very much about how human beings should relate to the natural environment and to the other sentient inhabitants of the natural environment.

Some similar points apply to the discourse of rights, which has some historical links with Kantian ethics. Of course, it is not difficult to argue for the importance of the recognition and institutionalisation of human rights in the modern world. Politically and legally this discourse is of immense importance, and it probably provides the best basis we have for building a sense of shared standards within a global ethical environment. Respect for other people's rights, taken seriously, is not a position of non-intervention; in this it may differ only in degree and in detail from a serious consequentialism that focuses on well-being. But the question 'what rights do other people have?', like Kantian questions about whether other people are being respected, will not take us very far in many of life's decisions. And in some areas of life it may be far from the most salient question to ask. Intimate personal relationships, for instance, including parent–child relationships, are not necessarily at their best when each decides what to do *primarily* by asking what the other has a right to, even though a recognition of the rights of the other is never redundant.

Chapter 3 considered whether the discourse of virtues might be superior to considerations drawn from ethical theories of right action when it comes to conceptualising the qualities to be developed through education. One point to be mentioned here is that the discourse of virtues itself allows for great internal diversity; we have already noted that different traditions of life may embody different virtues, and it may also be that different roles even within one society call for different virtues. (If we think that we need teachers, nurses, doctors, police officers, soldiers, politicians, bureaucrats, artists, technicians, engineers, scientists, and that all of these will play some role as citizens while many will be parents, how far will we be able to go in specifying one set of virtues that will be right for everyone?) Even if we find that we can say much of what we need to say about values education in the language of virtues, this does not imply that this language by itself could provide all that is needed in an ethical environment. Neither the assessment of consequences in terms of well-being, nor the claims of rights and justice, nor probably the moral claims we may feel obliged to make on behalf of animals and the natural environment, can be fully addressed through talk of human virtues.

If any one kind of ethical resource is insufficient in life as we know it now, there is no reason for confidence that a one-dimensional ethical environment could provide us with the resources to address problems that we cannot even envisage. From a social perspective, then, we have reason to hope that our ethical environment will not become impoverished. From a more individual perspective, we can recognise that an ethical environment as rich as the one available to us now offers many different ways in which individuals can find value and meaning in life.

One important implication of this is that both religious and a-religious[4] outlooks have a place in such an environment. There are those who believe that religion has, on balance, brought more harm than good to the world (besides promoting belief in falsehoods, which may or may not be thought to have negative value independently of the suffering produced). And there are those who believe that lack of religion (which perhaps, in an historical and global perspective, has been the minority tendency so far) is in the process of bringing more harm than good to the world (besides promoting lack of belief in fundamentally important truths). The question is not empirically decidable (in part because religious and a-religious perspectives will not entirely agree on what counts as harm and good). Even if it were empirically decidable, it would be a large step from there to concluding in favour of an entirely religious or entirely a-religious ethical environment. But what we can say is that the existence, and indeed interaction, of religious and non-religious perspectives enriches the ethical environment. In this respect, as in others, we should not see diversity within the ethical environment only as a matter of fact that education needs to take into account, though it certainly is that. We can also see it as something that we would all be worse off without.

5 Intervening in the ethical environment

If my argument in the previous chapter is correct, there are ways of sustaining or seeking to improve the ethical environment that can be taken (or taken effectively) only by government. Among the most obvious of these ways are interventions in schooling, such as the institution on a large scale, across a nation, of programmes of values education within the nation's publicly-funded schools. (While I am assuming here for convenience that the level of government in question is national, many of the same questions that need to be raised about intervention at this level would apply also to governmental intervention in the ethical environment at local, sub-national levels and also at international levels.) Can such interventions, intended to change the ethical environment, be legitimate? (The legitimacy in question, of course, is *moral* legitimacy, to borrow a phrase that draws on a law-like conception of morality.)

Brighouse (2004) recognises that education offers the most natural way for governments to intervene in the ethical environment (or, as he calls it, the ethos) of a society, and that to do this successfully is to influence the 'patterns of interpretation and evaluation' that 'manifest themselves in individuals' judgements and choices about how to live' (Brighouse 2004: 149).[1] He points out that 'governments typically do use their control over schooling in this manner' (2004: 149), citing the use of schooling to inculcate patriotic sentiment, to promote religious faith, or to promote democratic character. What Brighouse is asking, and what we need to ask here, is whether such educational interventions in the ethical environment can be legitimate. Since the underlying issues may not turn on education as such, but on more general questions about the relationship between the state and individuals, it is with the more general questions that we need to start.

The legitimacy of government intervention

There are several reasons for caution about the idea of governments seeking actively to intervene in the ethical environment. These reasons are themselves, of course, grounded in considerations already present within the ethical environment: many of them stem from a caution about the power of governments that is strong within broadly liberal-democratic traditions. An ethical environment that did not contain any grounds for suspicion about government intervening in that very environment would be to that extent a poorer ethical environment. But this does not mean that such intervention is wrong; it may be possible to answer the grounds for suspicion. Some of the considerations in question may seem less salient to readers who have not themselves been strongly influenced by such traditions. There is, however, at least one reason for caution that is not specific to a liberal tradition, because it pre-dates it: that there is little reason to trust either the ethical expertise or the probity of governments. Within any political system, members of governments are not necessarily motivated by concern for the welfare of those subject to the power of the government, or by any other moral purpose. Seeking power and the maintenance of power is always liable to be a strong motivation for many of those in government; possibilities of corruption can never be entirely eliminated.

To recognise such dangers in government is not yet to enter into a liberal-democratic way of thinking. Plato recognised the dangers but was by no means led towards a faith in democracy; rather, as he famously argued in *The Republic*, the only guarantee of good government would be that disinterested philosophers hold power. In modern political philosophy there is a *communi-tarian* strand that is sceptical of aspects of liberalism.[2] For the communitarian, roughly, a society is a good society to the extent that it constitutes a real community, where 'community' implies a substantial sharing of values and beliefs. Where this substantial sharing exists, it may more readily be *assumed* that a government drawn from and representing the same community will act in accordance with those values and beliefs. Perhaps the members of such a community would feel able to trust their government to uphold the quality of their ethical environment.

It would no doubt be easier to make an argument for the role of government in sustaining the ethical environment if one could start from communitarian premises. But to do that would be to beg too many questions. There are some strands of recent communitarian thinking that have rightly been influential among liberal philosophers. These include the recognition that belonging to a community and being able to identify with it are human goods in their own right, not to be neglected in the face of more individualistic values. The type of virtue ethics that emphasises the need for substantive conceptions of virtues to be rooted in particular traditions can also be seen as communitarian. But communitarianism is at its weakest as a *political* theory of the state. Whether we look to ethnicity, to religious belief, or to values expressed and lifestyle practised, it is doubtful whether any modern state is sufficiently homogeneous to count as including all its inhabitants within a single community in any substantial sense (whatever the image that some governments may wish to present). And even if the whole populace of a state did constitute a community, that would not by itself guarantee that those who gained power could be trusted to uphold the good of the whole community.

These considerations are, in effect, arguments for a liberal-democratic conception of the relation between individual and state. It would be superfluous here to go any further into the arguments that are part of the mainstream of political philosophy in the modern Western world. Concretely we can recognise that at least some strands of both liberal and democratic practice have been on the rise in recent years in many countries that cannot be considered, in geographical terms, part of the Western world. Where elements of greater individual choice come into social practices, and elements of greater democracy come into political practices, the changes are not necessarily driven by abstract ideas and values. The extension of choice and breaking down of traditional ways of doing things (in family life and in employment, for instance) may have more to do with the modernisation of economic life within a context of globalisation of trade, and the extension of opportunities of political participation may have more to do with gradually increasing levels of both material well-being and education. A desire for democracy is compatible with a wish to institutionalise democracy in homegrown ways rather than through a Western model being imported (or imposed). But whatever the explanation, it seems likely that arguments about the role of the state and the limits of state intervention that have been conducted within a liberal framework in the West will become increasingly salient in many countries. This seems, then, the appropriate framework within which to conduct the argument here.

It is within a liberal framework that Brighouse raises his question about the legitimacy of governmental interventions through schooling. He mentions three conditions that are all necessary if government action is be legitimate. First, the action must be such that reasonable people can consent to it. Second, many actual individuals must in fact consent to it (this is clearly a condition of *democratic* legitimacy). And third, the actual consent *must not have been manufactured*. If a government has ensured, through its programmes in schools, that people will consent to its policies, then we can question whether that consent gives any legitimacy to the government. In Brighouse's words, 'for consent to count, it has to be the result of the free and unmanipulated reasoning of the citizens themselves' (2004: 152). The government 'should not attempt to reach into and alter the motivational structure of the citizen without directly engaging his or her reason' (2004: 152). Brighouse recognises that by this argument 'such practices as using public education to promote patriotism, or even loyalty to civic institutions, can be problematic' (2004: 152).

Is there any more to be said? Can we perhaps find conditions under which educational programmes of intervention in the ethical environment can be legitimate? In exploring this question, the next section will set the scene by reference to one recent example of thinking about government strategy in England, and one classic work of liberal political philosophy: John Stuart Mill's *On Liberty*. Both refer to education; we can use Mill's discussion to raise questions about the kind of intervention favoured in the recent strategic report. The later sections of this chapter will take up in turn the issues of indoctrination, manipulation and autonomy.

A case study within a liberal ethical environment

Of the two texts that will be taken as reference points in this section, Mill's *On Liberty* (1975), written in the mid-nineteenth century, has indisputably been influential in modern liberal thinking. The second is a much more recent, and much less noticed, British discussion that has addressed some of the same root concerns within a twenty-first century context: a report from the UK Prime Minister's Strategy Unit (2004). This report, *Personal Responsibility and Changing Behaviour*, examines ways in which government can influence public behaviour for the better through increasing individuals' sense of responsibility for their own actions and choices. It has in common with Mill the recognition that there are many ways in which behaviour can be influenced and that it is important to ask which ways are morally desirable.

It may be helpful first to set out more systematically some of the broadly liberal reasons for caution about government intervention in the ethical environment.

- Such intervention requires judgements about the quality of the ethical environment. But government as such has no more expertise on such matters than anyone else, and may get the judgements wrong. While an individual's judgements about the quality of her surrounding ethical environment may have little public effect, there are substantial dangers in government getting its judgements wrong.

- Even if we assume that government can get the judgements right – and, further, that it can do something effective to uphold an ethical environment of the kind it judges best – this will inevitably have an impact on the way individuals live their lives, in some case constraining individual choices. But it may be seen as objectionable to constrain individual choices for the sake of the good of the society in general.

- An objection that tends in the same direction, though on a different basis, would have it, not that individual choices are being constrained for the good of the society, but that they are being constrained for individuals' own good. This may be objected to as paternalistic.

At this point we can look at what Mill said about intervention in people's lives (coming later to his thoughts specifically on education). At the heart of his argument was his 'harm principle': 'That the only purpose for which power can rightfully be exercised over any member of a civilised community, against his will, is to prevent harm to others. His own good, either physical or moral, is not a sufficient warrant' (Mill 1975: 15).

Though this principle, and its attribution to Mill, are hardly public knowledge in England or anywhere else, there is evidence that something not unlike it is implicit in much public opinion in England.[3] The Prime Minister's Strategy Unit, which draws on a wide range of empirical evidence, finds that 'broadly, the public recognises a legitimate role for the government to intervene where there are significant externalities to behaviour – i.e. individual behaviour creates costs or benefits for others', and it goes on to report that 'people seem more accepting of state intervention where externalities are negative' (p. 62) – in other words, where harm is liable to be caused to others.

Mill's brand of liberalism, with the harm principle at its heart, has often been taken to imply that, provided government protects individuals from harming each other, it has no business trying to make people more moral. But the idea of government trying to sustain or improve the ethical environment may sound as if it is trying to do just that, and since it is not directly about preventing people harming each other, it apparently violates the harm principle.

We need to proceed with some caution here. Rather than assuming that interventions in the ethical environment are not about preventing harm, we can start from a goal that clearly is about preventing harm, and show that interventions in the ethical environment can be a means of pursuing that goal. Then we can move on to consider whether such interventions become objectionable if they are not so clearly about preventing harm.

We can start, then, with the prevention of criminal behaviour. In societies that already have a long history of liberal influence, we can assume for the most part that behaviour is not criminal (not prohibited by the criminal law) unless there is a well-grounded presumption that it is harmful to others. In England, for instance, an argument over whether homosexual activity between consenting adults should be criminal was worked through in the 1960s (Devlin 1965; Hart 1963); the law was changed to make such acts no longer illegal, essentially by an appeal to liberal principles like Mill's. If changes in the ethical environment in this case followed the legal changes more than they preceded them, they are well entrenched by now. The predominant climate of opinion has moved from intolerance (institutionalised in criminality) through tolerance (which, strictly speaking, is accepting what you still take to be wrong) to an ethical acceptance (by no means unanimous) that no longer views the activity as wrong.

If, then, we look at activities that are now criminal, the presumption is that they are criminal because they involve harm to others. Sometimes, as we have seen in the case of laws against racial discrimination (which certainly causes harm to its victims) a wider change in what is publicly acceptable may follow changes in the law. But sometimes authorities have open to them ways of working on the ethical environment without changing the law itself. In Chapter 1 we noted the findings, associated with New York's 'broken windows' policy among other examples, that improving the physical environment can lead to changes in behaviour. This does not happen simply through a one-to-one influence of the environment on each individual; more importantly, it involves a change in what is accepted or not accepted, admired or found reprehensible, within a particular community or sub-culture; a changing and 'embedding of social norms', in the words of the Strategy Unit (p. 58). Indeed the Strategy Unit explicitly refers to the approach it recommends as an 'ecological' one (p. 16).

What of activity that may seem to be primarily self-regarding? Should government intervene to save people from endangering their own life, as in driving cars without seat belts, or smoking? Public attitudes on such matters vary over time and from one society to another. Part of the argument for intervention is, of course, that no such behaviour is purely self-regarding; even when it does not directly endanger others, it is liable to draw on publicly provided medical resources. In some cases making the behaviour criminal may be the best measure open to government; in other cases, as with smoking in England, government has used a mix of strategies – age-related restrictions on sales, health warnings, banning of advertising and education in schools on the dangers of smoking – none of which amounts to outright banning of the activity (at least for consenting adults in private), but which cumulatively do tend to change the public norms relating to smoking.

There are other cases again (not considered by the Strategy Unit) where educational measures may be the major ones through which a change in the ethical environment is attempted. England is one of those countries in which an explicit programme of education for citizenship has been a late arrival in the curriculum. When the government set up a Committee to make recommendations for citizenship education, it did so with the aim of addressing 'worrying levels of apathy, ignorance and cynicism about public life' (Advisory Group on Citizenship 1998: 7) which had been demonstrated in various ways including low turnouts in elections. The Committee in making its recommendations (which resulted in the incorporation of citizenship education into the National Curriculum) said that it aimed at 'no less than a change in the political culture of this country both nationally and locally: for people to think of themselves as active citizens' (Advisory Group on Citizenship 1998: 6). As the word 'culture' shows, the aim is not just to influence the thinking of each individual student who takes the programme; rather, the aim is that people should come to expect themselves *and others* to take part in running public affairs – that the social norms relating to political participation should change.

What would Mill have thought of such interventions? He was primarily concerned to limit the coercion that either the state *or public opinion* can exercise over individual behaviour. The very fact that he is concerned about public opinion shows that he is aware of the ethical environment and the power it can have. At times he speaks of public opinion as potentially tyrannical:

> Protection . . . against the tyranny of the magistrate is not enough: there needs protection also against the tyranny of the prevailing opinion and feeling; against the tendency of society to impose . . . its own ideas and practices as rules of conduct on those who dissent from them.
>
> Mill 1975: 9

At other times he clearly sees the potential for positive value in the ethical environment:

> Human beings owe to each other help to distinguish the better from the worse, and encouragement to choose the former and avoid the latter. They should be forever stimulating each other to increased exercise of their higher faculties, and increased direction of their feelings and aims towards wise instead of foolish, elevating instead of degrading, objects and contemplations.
>
> Mill 1975: 93

Is there a contradiction here? No, because Mill's point is that while we can, and should, seek to encourage people to seek what is good, and to do good towards others,[4] we should not actually *prevent* them doing what they wish and decide unless it is harmful to others. The application of his point turns on our being able to make two distinctions: both between what is harmful and what is not, and also between what is coercive prevention and what is only influence. We can be clear that the threat of penalties within the criminal law counts as coercion, but to draw the line within public opinion between what, on the one hand, leaves individuals free to follow or disregard generally accepted norms, and what, on the other hand, counts as constraint, is open to endless dispute (and has generated much scholarly debate since Mill's time). The difficulty of working with Mill's harm principle within the realm of public opinion may have contributed to the current ethical climate in England being, probably, a good deal more liberal and permissive than Mill himself would have liked. People in England are often unwilling actively to criticise what they privately think is reprehensible, let alone encourage others to do what they think to be good.

That disposition of 'live and let live' often holds in modern liberal societies of relations between adults. We may still think that we can, and should, seek to influence young people. The Strategy Unit is clear about one of the reasons for this: 'generally speaking it is thought that behaviours and habits are shaped early in life' (p. 64). In the light of that it is surprising that the Strategy Unit gives little weight to ways in which 'behaviours and habits' can be directly addressed in schools. While it does, in its section on schools (pp. 54–60), refer to strategies for addressing misbehaviour within schools, it does not consider any evidence as to whether such strategies have a longer-term effect.

Independently of the Strategy Unit, what should we think about deliberate attempts to influence the ethical environment through education? Mill himself would not have tried to apply the harm principle to schooling, since he says of the principle: 'this doctrine is meant to apply only to human beings in the maturity of their faculties. We are not speaking of children, or of young persons below the age which the law may fix as that of manhood or womanhood' (Mill 1975: 15).

Later, it becomes clear that Mill does think that adult society should work on the ethical environment through the influence it exercises over children:

> The existing generation is master both of the training and the entire circumstances of the generation to come; it cannot indeed make them perfectly wise and good, because it is itself so lamentably deficient in goodness and wisdom; and its best efforts are not always, in individual cases, its most successful ones; but it is perfectly well able to make

the rising generation, as a whole, as good as, and a little better than, itself.

Mill 1975: 101

As Mill goes on to point out, the very fact that adult society can influence the younger generation to this extent means that it should be quite unnecessary to coerce them for their own good once they are adults. But while he acknowledges the importance of adult influence, he did not want that influence to be centralised in the State: 'A general State education is a mere contrivance for moulding people to be exactly like one another: and as the mould in which it casts them is that which pleases the predominant power in the government ... it establishes a despotism over the mind' (Mill 1975: 130).

So Mill would have been wary when the claim that 'behaviour is most powerfully shaped when all the influences on a young person, from infancy to adulthood, point in the same direction' (Strategy Unit: 64) comes from a department of government. Such a claim may bring to mind notions of Jesuit upbringing, of conditioning, of indoctrination. It is characteristic of modern liberal educational discourse that such notions are bogies, labels liable to be used when threats are perceived to the autonomy that (correspondingly) is held up as a central educational value. So we need to look carefully at whether an attempt to work on our shared ethical environment by deliberate educational measures could amount to indoctrination, or could be a significant infringement on autonomy.

Indoctrination

A few decades ago, much of the time of philosophers of education in the English-speaking academic world was directed at the clarification of individual education-related concepts. Sometimes the preferred method of clarification was to seek a definition of a term that would give necessary and sufficient conditions for its correct use. One term that received this treatment in a considerable number of articles (many collected in Snook 1972) was 'indoctrination'. No consensus on the meaning of the term was reached. We can see why the term is difficult to tie down by looking briefly at some of the suggested answers to the question: what has to be the case if we are to be able correctly to identify cases of indoctrination?

One possibility is that indoctrination must involve a *doctrine*, where a doctrine is not an isolated belief but a system of beliefs that have a bearing on how people live their lives. It would not be plausible to suggest that no one can hold a doctrine without being indoctrinated, so the criterion of a doctrine being involved at least has to be supplemented by some reference to the manner in which it is held or how it comes to be held. We shall come to those issues in a moment. But even if it is agreed that a person who has been indoctrinated must hold a doctrine of some sort, there is ample room for dispute over just what kind of belief system will count as a doctrine.

Religion may furnish the most obvious cases (partly because religious believers will sometimes willingly use the term 'doctrine' for elements of their own beliefs), but there are other belief systems whose status as doctrines may be asserted by some and disputed by others. The systems in question will be characterised in part by their involving both normative assumptions and assumptions that appear to be factual assertions but may actually be untestable. Candidates include certain systematic bodies of political theory such as Marxism, and certain systematic bodies of scientific theory (which their critics would claim to be pseudo-scientific) including psychoanalytic theory and Darwinian evolution. A case can also be made that there are still more all-embracing worldviews, outside the scope of religion, that have the status of doctrines: perhaps the enterprise of science itself, resting on presuppositions about predictability and testability that cannot themselves be tested; or perhaps a materialistic worldview whose ruling out of religious claims is itself a matter of faith rather than evidence. The point here is *not* that all of these instances should be counted as doctrines (perhaps any of them *could* be held in a way that is not doctrinal) but only that reference to doctrines is inconclusive in any attempt to clarify which actual phenomena count as indoctrination.

Perhaps we should turn from questions about the kind of belief that is held in cases of indoctrination, to questions about the *way* in which indoctrinated beliefs are held. It is commonly suggested that an indoctrinated belief is immune from critical reflection; the person who is indoctrinated will be impervious to counterargument or contrary evidence. That view identifies indoctrination primarily as a certain cognitive and perhaps also affective condition (affective because an emotional resistance may be part of the explanation for the immunity from critical reflection) – a state of mind.

It is also possible to see indoctrination as an activity in which certain people engage. Commonly, if we think someone has been indoctrinated we presuppose that some person or agency has been responsible for bringing this about. Assuming for the moment that this presupposition is correct, what has to be true of someone if they are engaging in indoctrination? Is there some particular method they must be following? It is sometimes suggested that non-rational methods of transmitting beliefs are constitutive of indoctrination, but this faces the problem that we may get young children to hold various beliefs (for instance, that 2 + 2 equals 4) in ways that do not proceed through any kind of rational argument. It may not be possible to identify any specific method that constitutes indoctrination; instead, it may be that an indoctrinator will be willing to use any method that does the job. That suggestion puts the weight again on a certain outcome – namely, as above, that someone's belief is immune from critical reflection – but holds that indoctrination, as a process, is taking place when someone is intentionally taking action to bring about that outcome.

But does indoctrination have to be a process deliberately undertaken by someone? Or is it possible that the activity of a teacher who intends to bring about a rationally held belief could inadvertently result in a condition of immunity to rational reflection? Could indoctrination come about accidentally?

By this point we might reasonably wonder whether the attempt to find a definitive criterion of indoctrination is misplaced. As a part of ordinary language rather than a technical term, the word is hardly likely to be susceptible to precise definition in terms of necessary and sufficient conditions. Rather, it gets it meaning from its use, and the context of its use is a certain kind of ethical environment. Within a broadly liberal environment, the notion of indoctrination serves to direct our attention to certain concerns and worries. Rather than trying, as if in a value-free context, to clarify the meaning of a word, it will be more helpful to ask what it is that we are, or should be, worried about in cases where we might suspect indoctrination.

The attentions of analytical philosophers of education, when discussing indoctrination, have mostly focused on what it is that an individual (who is indoctrinating someone) does, or what it is that has happened to an individual who has been indoctrinated. As often, we may find an illuminatingly different perspective if we look instead at the environment. It was an Hungarian philosopher of education (Horvath 1991), writing only shortly after the collapse of communism, who perhaps first brought the environmental focus into the philosophical analysis of indoctrination, seeing it as a 'cultural phenomenon' (1991: 57). He wrote:

> Indoctrination is effective when the scope of values, concepts and meanings or, in general terms, of the elements of social discourse narrows. It works when people ask fewer and fewer questions not because it is forbidden (that would be sheer aggressive oppression) but because the list of questionable things is curtailed. More and more things in society are taken for granted or unalterably set.
>
> Horvath 1991: 55

If that is what happens when indoctrination works, what should we say that it *is*? For Horvath, 'it is the deliberate action of changing and increasing the number of unquestioned things in a given culture' (1991: 55). In this view, then, there are still agents – the authorities, politicians, perhaps also some of the intellectuals and teachers – intentionally aiming at bringing about the narrowing of discourse. This would allow us to say, in terms Brighouse uses, that 'manipulation of the ethos' (Brighouse 2004: 153) is going on, and that consent, in so far as there is consent at all, is being manufactured. We should note two further points: first, as Horvath observes, that the intention is by no means always successful, as demonstrated by the fact that in the late 1980s many critical minds did rapidly emerge in Eastern Europe. And second, that what should most worry us, presumably, is the condition of society itself – whether it is one where the list of unquestionable things is narrow – rather than the issue (which Horvath points out could be very hard to settle empirically) – of whether some agency has been *intentionally* bringing about that condition.

Why is it bad for the range of questionable things in a culture to be narrower than it need be? One answer would again refer directly to the condition of individuals: that corresponding to a narrowness in the scope of 'values, concepts and meanings' that are available to an individual there is a narrowing of the individual's autonomy. We shall return to the idea of autonomy below. There is another answer in terms of environmental factors: that a culture that is narrower in its values, concepts and meanings is a less diverse environment, and that diversity within an ethical environment is itself desirable (a point independently argued at the end of the previous chapter).

In this consideration of indoctrination we have come in effect to a comparison of two kinds of ethical environment. In one (such as that in communist Hungary described by Horvath) the range of discourse about values is limited, but in so far as people are confined within that environment they do not realise how limited it is. Interestingly, Horvath points out that in Hungarian there is no word for 'indoctrination': this in itself would have made it more difficult to mount the kind of critique that Horvath (accustomed to Anglophone philosophy of education) could make. The other ethical environment in the comparison is a liberal one, in which many things can be questioned, in which education to some degree encourages questioning, and in which the notion of indoctrination as something to be avoided is itself salient. In the latter kind of environment indoctrination (on any interpretation within the range indicated above) is less likely to take place, for three interrelated reasons. First, where many things can be questioned, and where at least to some degree education encourages questioning, more questioning will tend to go on, and young people will be initiated into an environment in which things are questioned. So it is less likely that they will assimilate what they are told or even what is most prevalent in their surroundings uncritically.

Second, in such an environment there will in fact be a plurality of points of view, so that young people almost inevitably will become aware that there are alternative positions to those into which they have been inducted; in other words, it is not just that a certain disposition to ask questions will be encouraged in the abstract, but that the concrete existence of alternatives will present itself. The third reason becomes pertinent if, despite the more general environmental factors of the existence of alternatives and the encouragement of questioning, somebody still attempts deliberately to indoctrinate. The very existence within such an environment of the notion of indoctrination as something to be wary of makes it less likely that deliberate indoctrination (which of its nature will have to be somewhat surreptitious) will go undetected.

The upshot so far is that attempts by government to bring about or sustain a particular quality of ethical environment need be in no way indoctrinatory if the kind of environment to be encouraged is itself one in which many things can be questioned. A concrete instance is provided by the work of the English Advisory Group on Citizenship mentioned above. Its stated aim, as we saw, was to produce people who would think of themselves as active citizens, and it went on to say that these would be people 'willing, able and equipped to have an influence in public life and with the critical capacities to weigh evidence before speaking and acting' (Advisory Group on Citizenship 1998: 7). The aim, then, is to develop just those capacities and dispositions that would be antithetical to indoctrination. Yet it has to be said that the reality of practice can diverge from the stated aim, so that there is still a need for caution.

Manipulation

If we would object to indoctrination on the grounds that it limits an individual's autonomy, this suggests that the positive value put on autonomy is more fundamental than the negative value put on indoctrination. If that is so, then we should consider whether there are other ways in which autonomy can be undermined, besides indoctrination. Might it be (as suggested on occasion by Brighouse's language) that government attempts to create or sustain a certain kind of ethical environment are manipulative, even if they do not involve indoctrination? We can understand manipulation in relation to the Kantian principle of never treating others purely as a means to your own ends, which, as we saw in Chapter 3, is one of the formulations of his categorical imperative.

If government seeks to use education as a route towards sustaining the ethical environment, it will be seeking to influence that environment *through* the influence that is exerted on individuals as part of their education (we shall see more in the next chapter of the forms this influence may take). Is that not a case of using individuals for a social end? In normal life it *could* be said that we constantly use other people towards our ends (if we would usually resist saying this, it is because the very notion of 'using' someone has such negative connotations in a liberal environment). Where this can be done in a way that is compatible with respecting those persons, we are not treating them *solely* as means towards our own ends. Whenever we engage, for instance, in any commercial transaction to acquire goods or services we are making use of the labour of those who have been instrumental in producing or providing the goods or services. We normally assume that this is not illegitimate, not incompatible with respect for persons, because those others have consented to their labour being used in such ways. Where this is not the case we might, within a different discourse from Kant's, speak of exploitation. In Kantian terms (Kant 1785: 92) the test of illegitimate use of another is whether the other has or could have consented to being used towards the particular end in question. What is wrong, for instance, with making a promise that we have no intention of keeping, is that in doing so we have to conceal from the person to whom we make the promise what our real end is (e.g. to get money without having to pay it back), since the other could not possibly share that end. Had we revealed our true intention, they would not have consented.

If this captures roughly what we mean by 'manipulation', then we have to consider whether a government policy aimed at sustaining the quality of the ethical environment through influencing individuals could amount to manipulation. We might ask, first, whether the individual concerned would or reasonably could give their consent to the policy if they fully understood it. The problem with this in any practical political context, as Brighouse (2004: 152) makes clear, is that it is too easy for governments to avail themselves of the argument that people *would* consent if they were reasonable and fully understood the policy in question. That is part of the reason why liberal politics has historically come to be linked with democracy, since democracy provides a way, whatever its imperfections in practice, of allowing actual rather than merely hypothetical consent to be registered. Yet the fact that a government has been democratically elected does not remove the possibility of manufactured consent, hence of manipulation. If a government, perhaps through a variety of processes including educational ones, succeeds in changing the ethical environment in such a way that people do not realise that the changes have been brought about by government, then we might well think that people have been manipulated. They have been brought, perhaps by an imperceptibly gradual process, to go along with something that they might not have consented to had they been fully aware of what was happening.

The report of the Prime Minister's Strategy Unit referred to above shows some awareness of this issue, but perhaps not enough. Recall that the Strategy

Unit proposes using an ecological approach to bring about changes in people's behaviour, not primarily through direct means such as instituting incentives or penalties, or through public information campaigns (using announcements and advertisements that, short of being totally subliminal, can have no effect without people being aware of them) but through more subtle means that may gradually change social norms.

The Report comments:

> In many cases there may be a need for public debate to establish a consensus behind new policies to promote behaviour change. In highly individualistic societies, which place a high premium on personal autonomy, it is vital that there is wide understanding of the need for any policies focused on behaviour change. Otherwise they are likely to be seen as illegitimate – and as a result less effective.
>
> Prime Minister's Strategy Unit 2004: 63

Notice that the Report does not say that policies introduced without wide public understanding *would* be illegitimate – only that they are likely to be seen as illegitimate, and consequently to be less effective (as well as, though this is not mentioned, more threatening to the governing party's majority). Thus the task from government's point of view is an instrumental one: for the sake of effectiveness, policies need to be seen as legitimate; for the sake of being seen as legitimate, a public debate is needed *to establish a consensus.* The possibility that the debate might result in a lack of consensus, or in a consensus against the policy proposed, is not considered here. It is easy to imagine this line of argument being pursued within a political system that is not fundamentally democratic at all. As expressed here, it does appear manipulative.

It may be that governments often do say, when they already intend to bring in a certain policy that they suspect will meet initial resistance, that a public debate is needed. But a fully democratic system does not need public debate only 'in many cases', where the cases for debate are selected by government. It needs the permanent possibility of debate, together with the possibility of the debate making a real difference. If the possibility of manipulation is to be minimised, citizens need to be aware of the channels for debate, and they need to know that government has open to it channels for influencing the ethical environment that are more subtle than overt incentives, penalties or exhortations. To ensure that they have this knowledge will itself be an important task for education – one to which we shall return in the next chapter.

Autonomy

It was suggested above that a positive valuation of autonomy underlies the negative valuation put on both indoctrination and manipulation. In Chapter 3 it was argued that both the importance of promoting autonomy and the likelihood of success in promoting it are dependent on the surrounding ethical environment. Raz argues that in societies 'whose social forms are to a considerable extent based on individual choice' (Raz 1986: 394) autonomy is an essential condition of a good life. 'For those who live in an autonomy-supporting environment there is no choice but to be autonomous. There is no other way to prosper in such a society' (Raz 1986: 391).

If one accepts Raz's claim, it is easy to conclude that education should promote autonomy, as a condition of a good life (cf. White 1991). But the matter is not so straightforward in plural societies. As noted in Chapter 3, there are traditions in which some parents will attach little importance to their children growing up as autonomous critical thinkers. These parents, and the communities with which they identify, may think that the promotion of autonomy will undermine the firm commitment to a traditional framework of beliefs and values that they (the parents) are trying to instil into their children. (The notion of autonomy here is being taken to denote more than the degree of independence demanded in modern societies for passing an exam, getting a job, and so on; it refers to a more general capacity and disposition for critical and questioning thought.)

Political philosophers discussing liberal and plural societies are divided on whether the state should through education seek to promote autonomy. In response to a number of philosophers who have argued for autonomy-promoting education (such as Gutmann 1987), Brighouse has argued that the liberal state should institutionalise only an autonomy-facilitating education (Brighouse 2000: 65–82). Such an education would not teach that autonomy is a virtue desirable in its own right; rather, it would teach 'autonomy-related skills' (Brighouse 2000: 69). Brighouse's 'recommendations favour knowledge and skills over virtue' (2000: 80). He explains:

> The education does not try to ensure that students employ autonomy in their own lives, any more than Latin classes are aimed at ensuring that students employ Latin in their lives. Rather it aims to enable them to live autonomously should they wish to, rather as we aim to enable them to criticise poetry, do algebra, etc. without trying to ensure that they do so.
>
> Brighouse 2000: 80

If Brighouse's treatment of autonomy as a set of skills is reasonable, then it should allay the worries of any communities who may prefer their children not to lead their lives autonomously, since it does not try to ensure that they will live that way. But there are problems with Brighouse's interpretation of autonomy. First, it is doubtful that the teaching of any skills in school is value-neutral in the way Brighouse implies. Good teachers, of Latin, algebra, or any other subject, are likely to convey a degree of enthusiasm for their subject, and hence a sense that the subject is worth doing. This is partly because a teacher who has no enthusiasm for a subject is likely to teach it less well, and partly because students are less likely to learn how to do a subject if they do not themselves come to see it as worthwhile, and come to care about doing it well.

Second, Brighouse misrepresents the nature of autonomy by comparing it with subjects such as Latin or algebra, which are not essential to everyone in modern life. A closer analogy would be with skills in the use of the major first language in one's society, or in arithmetical aspects of numeracy. Not being able to use English well in an English-speaking society or not having some basic level of numeracy *are* drawbacks in modern life; teaching of these skills will generally (and rightly) try not merely to give people a skill which they can use if they so wish, but to develop the disposition to use the skill in circumstances in which it is appropriate. One might indeed consider that the teaching of arithmetic has hardly succeeded if an individual who *could* do accurate calculations if she tried does not actually realise when accuracy matters or care about accuracy when it does matter. Raz is closer to capturing the special status of autonomy when he criticises those who treat it as just one option among others: 'Their mistake is in disregarding the degree to which the condition of autonomy concerns a central aspect of the whole system of values of a society, which affects its general character' (Raz 1986: 394).

Third, and reinforcing Raz's point, the workings of justice in modern societies, including the criminal justice system, presuppose that people are not merely capable of making their own decisions about how to behave, but do in fact exercise that capacity. It would be no defence against criminal responsibility to claim that, while one had acquired autonomy-related skills, one did not choose to use them. Arguably it is unfair for the state to impose a criminal justice system that assumes autonomy if the state does not also take steps to ensure that people are disposed to exercise autonomy when it is called for.

That argument has some affinity to one made by Curren (2000), about the conditions under which the law can have legitimate jurisdiction over a person. It will not have legitimate jurisdiction, according to Curren, if 'the conditions for one's giving rational consent to the law' (Curren 2000: 179) are not met. Rational consent cannot be entirely non-autonomous consent, just as a decision for which one can be held responsible by the law cannot be entirely non-autonomous. But it is clear that the weight of such arguments depends heavily on just how autonomy is interpreted, how much is written into the notion. A number of writers have found it necessary to make distinctions within the broad concept of autonomy; White (1991), for instance, distinguishes weaker and stronger senses of 'personal autonomy', and there is some relationship between this and Benn's (1988) distinction between 'autarchy' and 'autonomy' where autarchy is weaker. Space does not permit here the detailed discussion that would be necessary for any thorough clarification of the notion of autonomy. But it can be suggested, again, that some guidance for the practice of education can be gained by focusing on the environment rather than on the precise conditions of autonomy in an individual.

Raz is surely right that societies that are broadly liberal, democratic and plural are autonomy supporting, and perhaps we should say also that they are autonomy demanding. A corollary of that is that the influences that exert pressure towards the attainment and exercise of autonomy are by no means to be found only within schools. Exposure to the wider culture and its political and institutional structure, awareness through mass media of alternative lifestyles and beliefs, experiences of differences in behaviour within a person's peer group, will all tend to show to young people how far autonomy is valued and practised within a society. To the extent that this is so, it will be the less necessary for schools positively to promote autonomy, as opposed to facilitating it. Maintaining the general autonomy-supporting environment, and ensuring that people have the skills to benefit from it, will be complementary aims for state policy; but if those aims are in place, it will not be essential to aim also at ensuring that every individual exercises autonomy to the full extent of his or her capacity. So long as we focus on autonomy as an element of an individual good life, then we must (on pain of inconsistency or at least inequity) seek to ensure it for all; but if the aim is the maintenance of an autonomy-supporting environment, there can be some latitude in how fully autonomy is realised for each individual.

An autonomy-supporting environment makes indoctrination less likely, as we saw above. Nevertheless, the same society that supports autonomy cannot completely rule out the possibility of indoctrination, since its liberal institutions leave a good deal of freedom to families, communities and institutions to pursue their own goals. A liberal society cannot guarantee that some families, communities or institutions will not set out to indoctrinate their own members in, say, fanatical beliefs and commitments that may be dangerous to the wider society. But it can seek to maintain the diversity and openness that make it difficult for any individuals not to be exposed to alternatives and to the example of criticism.

Within broadly liberal societies a greater threat to autonomy than deliberate indoctrination is that the ethical environment will come to be largely one-dimensional (to use the term introduced in the previous chapter); that certain assumptions about what is right and what is worthwhile in life will come to dominate public discourse, so that for individuals it will be much easier to go along with the general tide of opinion rather than critically reflecting on it. Going along with the general tide of opinion, even doing something because it is what everyone else does, is not necessarily bad in its consequences – that depends on what it is that everyone else does. Wanting to identify with like-minded others, wanting to be part of a society in which things are done in a certain way and in which certain values and assumptions hold sway, can be good – if the society is a good one of which to be a member. That shows again why the quality of the ethical environment is important, and also why it is important for individuals to have a sufficient degree of autonomy to be able to reflect on their ethical environment so that they are not just going along with it by default.

Democracy, diversity and education

If the arguments of this chapter are right, then it is possible for a government to intervene in the ethical environment, taking deliberate steps to try to secure or maintain a certain sort of environment, without offending against Mill's harm principle, without indoctrinating, without manipulating. But the *possibility* of this does not settle two important questions that can be raised in any actual case. First, is there sufficient security against the government actually engaging in indoctrinatory or manipulative measures? Second, is there any reason for trusting the government's evaluations of the quality of the ethical environment? Both questions are needed, because even if a government is able, in effect, to lead people in a certain direction by means that are legitimate, it may still be leading them in a mistaken direction.

The practical response to both points has to lie in democracy and diversity, and in the kind of education that can support both of those. The openness of government to scrutiny, which is part of democratic practice and institutions when they are working well, is necessary to guard against government's use of illegitimate means. And diversity of perspectives within a population is necessary if a governmental perspective is not to be allowed too easily to dominate public discourse. As for whether the government's perspective on the quality of the ethical environment is to be trusted, we have to recall the point made much earlier in this chapter, that there is no good reason to trust the ethical expertise or probity of a government just because it is the government.

It may be possible to find standards – perhaps those suggested at the end of the previous chapter – that could constrain a government's thinking about what kind of ethical environment is desirable. The application of those standards will still be legitimate only to the extent that there is some broader understanding of and consensus on them (that point already has implications for education that we shall follow up in the next chapter). And even if there were consensus at that level, there would be ample room for controversy over how well particular developments would meet those standards. A corollary of the value of diversity, argued for at the end of the previous chapter, is the desirability of lively public debate. That puts a heavy responsibility on education to see that people are prepared for such debate.

6 The responsibilities of values education

I argued in Chapter 4 that responsibilities for the ethical environment are widely distributed; they are not confined to schools. In the Conclusion I shall briefly return to some of those wider responsibilities. But schools are, of course, a major channel through which societal responsibilities can be exercised, and in this chapter I shall concentrate on what schools can and should do. In the process I shall revisit and expand on a number of points about values education that have been anticipated in earlier chapters. As indicated in the Introduction and at the beginning of Chapter 3, I am using the term 'values education' as a shorthand way of referring to all those tasks that schools should undertake in relation to values.

The previous two chapters have been concerned with large-scale questions about the quality of the ethical environment and the extent of governmental responsibility for it. In this chapter my focus will be more on how the ethical environment impinges on the individual. In the first section I shall introduce the idea that schools need to help individuals to find their way through the complexities and demands that they face within the ethical environment, and I shall answer the objection that to do this might be the responsibility of parents, not of schools. The next section will show why our contemporary ethical environment, by putting so much weight on individual choice, makes the task of helping young people to find their way through this environment especially compelling.

The later sections of the chapter will look at several of the ways in which schools, and the structure and content of schooling, have an impact on the ethical environment and on individuals' ability to cope with it. I shall raise some questions both about what kind of internal environment is desirable within a school, and about the desirability of diversity within the large-scale environment of the school system. Then I shall turn to questions about the curriculum, and say something more particularly about the role both of education about religion, and of education for citizenship. I shall end this chapter by re-emphasising that the exercise of the responsibilities of values education cannot be the preserve of any one part of the curriculum or indeed of any one aspect of schooling.

The individual in the ethical environment

The starting point in this chapter is a descriptive truth about education. All education tends to reproduce, even if it also in some respects changes, the ethical environment. This is another, and arguably better, way of expressing the sociological observation that education has the function of *transmitting values*. The term 'function' here is used descriptively, picking out one way in which education tends to maintain a social system; it recognises that no society or culture can retain its identity beyond one generation without passing on at least some of its core values. There is no implication that the particular set of values passed on is desirable. Even at this descriptive level, the terminology of the ethical environment is not redundant. The notion of transmitting values may convey too atomistic and mechanical a picture of what is going on, as if there are certain discrete values, which could be itemised, each of which may be more or less successfully passed on to this or that individual. The ethical environment, in contrast, is ongoing; what happens within education in relation to values is already within the ethical environment, not occupying some position outside it. Short of being totally removed from human society, it is impossible for individuals not to be inducted into an ethical environment of some sort, and formal education is just one of many processes by which that happens.

While formal education may contribute to a variety of social aims – an actively democratic society, an economically prosperous society, and so on – it makes its contribution primarily through the influence it has on individuals. If one social aim is to sustain a healthy ethical environment, schools can help to realise that aim through influencing the way that individuals learn to relate to their ethical environment. One way to get a grasp on the tasks of values education is by seeing what has to be involved in enabling individuals to find their way through their ethical environment. To find their way through it, individuals need to learn about it and reflect on it; in reflecting on it, they will become able to see the extent to which they will share in responsibility for the quality of that environment. There is, then, no contradiction between the social aim of sustaining the ethical environment and the individual aim of enabling individuals to understand and find their way through that environment; rather, these aims are complementary.

Before looking in detail at the contribution schools can make, there is a possible objection to be anticipated that can arise within some kinds of liberal perspective. Some would argue that any values-related education should not be mandated by government: that the place for education in values is in the family or in religious communities. A response to that has in effect been given in Chapters 4 and 5: the responsibility that we all have for the quality of our ethical environment cannot be exercised purely on a parent-to-child basis; in some respects it can only be exercised collectively. If we focus on the individual child, it will seem obvious to some that it is the child's parents who should be inculcating values. Suppose we put on one side any worries about the possibility of parents indoctrinating their children or inculcating values that seem to others undesirable (for we might also be worried about the state doing the same). Nevertheless, if we put due weight on the importance of the ethical environment on which the quality of life of all is in many ways dependent, then the idea that the responsibility should rest solely with parents is too *demanding*.

This is clearest in relation to the kind of large-scale social aims to which I shall return below, such as maintaining diversity within the ethical environment and promoting not just tolerance but understanding and respect. If these are goods for society, then a policy of leaving the relevant educational measures entirely to parents in relation to their own children would have to be supported by very good evidence that this would be the most effective way of proceeding. In the absence of such evidence, such a policy would seem more like a dereliction of responsibility on the part of government. But we can also focus on what the individual child needs from values education. Here the argument may be made that parents in their closeness to the child have a better view of the child's needs. Interestingly, such an argument is not often accepted in relation to academic aspects of the curriculum. From Mill onwards the argument has been made even in liberal environments that, if not for the good of society overall, then for the sake of the child, in case his or her parents do not fulfil their responsibilities, the State should seek to 'make the universal acquisition, and what is more, retention, of a certain minimum of general knowledge, virtually compulsory' (Mill 1975: 131). We do not usually expect parents to exercise their own judgement about which subjects a child should study or what the detailed content should be within those subjects. Is it more reasonable to expect parents to judge what their child needs in the area of values education?

To answer that we only need to look at the position of any individual child in relation to the ethical environment. When we realise how complex is the ethical environment that children face, and the range of knowledge and understanding that people need if they are to be able to find their way through that environment, it will be clear that it would be unreasonable to leave to parents the sole responsibility for that aspect of education. In societies that expect people to make their own decisions at many points in life, equipping them with the understanding they need in order to make those decisions and lead their own lives should be a public responsibility.

An environment of choice

Any person in a modern society faces a complex web of standards, expectations, opinions and aspirations that make up an enormously rich ethical environment. While this richness across a society is to be welcomed (if the arguments of earlier chapters are correct), it does bring costs as well as a multitude of possibilities for individuals. It is not desirable that very young children should be immediately exposed to the whole range of diversity within the environment; a degree of *cultural coherence* (Ackerman 1980: 141) is essential in the early years. But once they leave the immediate coherence that they may (if reasonably fortunate) find in home life, children have to start making sense of the greater diversity they encounter.

A rich ethical environment is one in which, because there are many possibilities, there are many choices and decisions to be made. Analyses of contemporary society (in affluent countries) that explore consumerism, marketisation and the consequent expanding role of choice, are not hard to come by (among the most recent examples, from a variety of perspectives, are Sacks 2002: Ch. 8; Schwartz 2004; Bottery 2004: Ch. 4). We do not need to add to such analyses here, but only to recall the variety of ways in which the range of choice facing individuals is expanding. We can start with goods that are available on the market in a traditional way.

As international trade and manufacturing capacity increase, the sheer variety of goods on the market, from foodstuffs to consumer durables, increases. And for many people, as disposable income increases, there is greater purchasing capacity. Access to a greater range of choices, often seen as a positive development, can itself make the process of choosing more difficult. So far, since we are not talking about any new *kind* of commodification, it may seem (if we are not opposed to the market as such) that ethical issues are in the background. But already the ethical environment comes into the picture in at least two ways. First, there is a familiar complaint about consumerism (which in this respect is seen as virtually equating with 'materialism'): that the endless preoccupation with getting and spending can come to eclipse other concerns in life, thereby providing a distinctive and arguably narrow perspective on 'the good life'. If that is too sweeping, and it is granted that being a consumer is only one department of life, a second point still applies. There are ethical pressures on consumer choices. Take food as an unavoidable area of consumption. Should food be organic, for the sake of the natural environment? Or is it better for the environment to avoid organic food that has been imported over long distances, in favour of that which is produced locally, by whatever methods? Should food be fair trade, for the sake of justice to the producers? Should a diet be wholly vegetarian, for the sake of animal welfare? Should the food that parents buy for their children (let alone for themselves) be always low in fat and salt for the sake of long-term health? Further issues arise in relation to clothing: is it produced by low-paid workers in a developing country? If so, is that a negative or positive contribution to the economy of the country in the long term? Or in relation to international travel: what does it do for the local economy? What does it do to the natural environment? And in relation to consumer durables: are they energy efficient?

Consumers are increasingly becoming aware of such issues. And if the questions have any force at all, consumers *should* be aware of them. There is at least, then, a *prima facie* case for schools to take a role for preparing consumers to take such issues into account. Ensuring that young people become aware of the issues, that they have access to relevant knowledge and understanding, and the opportunity to examine the issues, can best be seen as a public responsibility.

This is still only the beginning of the catalogue of choices that face people in modern societies. It is another familiar point that even in countries that have a strong tradition of welfare provision by the state, such central life concerns as schooling, health care and pensions, are opening up more and more of this provision to choice (and that this often will be called *consumer* choice). Sometimes the choice is between sources of provision – different schools, different hospitals – while costs are still covered from taxation. Sometimes, and increasingly, what used to be public services are opened up to commercial competition, so that rather than there being, say, one centralised provider of electricity or of rail services, the consumer is expected to choose. This is not the place to examine the arguments made for marketisation in terms of efficiency; the point to note here is simply the additional weight put on individual choice, which for some will be experienced as a burden. Where the necessity for individual choice is itself the result of public policy, we could reasonably expect that the same policy should do something, through public education, to enable people to cope with that choice.

The process of commodification is perhaps at its most striking when politics is seen as a matter of consumer choice (it could be argued that this goes back as far as Schumpeter 1950), in which political parties offer benefits to the voter in order to attract their vote. There is even an internationalised variant on this idea, in which individuals would be able to 'buy into' the country with the political and economic regime that best suits them (Davidson and

Rees-Mogg 1999, cited by Bottery 2004: 75). This is a very different picture of citizenship from that offered (though perhaps not often realised) by a participatory conception of democracy that looks not to individual choice but to deliberation yielding shared decisions with which all can identify (Fishkin and Laslett 2003). For any individual faced with a consumer choice between political parties there is a second-order and less obvious choice: whether to go along with the consumer model of citizenship by voting for the package that offers the best economic return; or to stay out of the market on the grounds that it will not make much difference (that many individuals have, more or less consciously, made this choice is one possible explanation of the perceived apathy about politics that, ironically, has often motivated politicians to invest in programmes of citizenship education); or to seek, against the tide, a more active and collective involvement in public affairs.

No one is only a consumer or only a citizen (unless we understand citizenship in a very broad sense – a point on which more will be said below). All have the potential for personal relationships; almost all are already members of some sort of family as they grow up and have the possibility of extending their family or starting a new family. (The different expressions here reflect rather different conceptions of the nature of the family: if we think of a family as extending across generations, then a new generation extends it further; but it is common in some cultures today to speak of a couple 'starting a family', as if making a new beginning.) Here certain patterns that might once have been taken for granted are now up for choice. One commentator has said:

> The great shibboleths of western family life have been dismantled: sex and marriage used to be interlinked – as did marriage and children, as did heterosexuality and marriage. Those links have been broken and people can assemble the bits as they wish: the worth accorded to individual autonomy has hugely increased and will continue to grow.
>
> Bunting 2004: 6

Though many parents may wish that their children were not growing up in such conditions, wishing will not change the conditions. That is not to claim that our present ethical environment is unalterable; the opposite has been argued here. But it is to recognise the limits of individual influence. To give a child no understanding of the range of opportunities, choices and risks that their society actually makes available, in matters of personal relationships as in others, would be to fail to prepare the child for the environment they will actually be entering.

The notion that what used to be given is now a matter of choice has perhaps been pushed furthest in the idea that people can choose their identity. There are problems in trying to take this expression literally: if choosing is being done it seems there must be some subject to do the choosing, but who is this subject if it is identity itself that is being chosen? But it is quite intelligible that many individuals in pluralistic societies have a diverse cultural inheritance. A person cannot choose to have been brought up in a certain cultural milieu in a certain place by certain parents and so on, but does have some scope in living out or playing down various elements of her cultural inheritance and her surroundings. Some young people may make a commitment to a parental tradition; some may compartmentalise, effectively living as one kind of person in the home and another in school or in social life; some may manage a kind of integration of disparate elements (Waldron 1996). In the process what might for a previous generation have been a matter of course (the son of a factory worker following his father into the job; the daughter of a Muslim family adopting Islamic dress) becomes something that, in awareness of alternatives, is consciously followed or not followed.

For many young people, though more in some societies than in others, such working out of how to live takes place in a context of religion. The idea of religion as an object of choice needs to be treated with caution for at least two reasons. One is that belief as such is not the sort of object that can be chosen; one can to some extent choose to pay or not pay attention to certain ideas, but one cannot, just like that, choose to believe something. Nevertheless, for many people there is increasingly a choice to engage or not engage in the practice of a religion (attendance at worship, enactment of rituals, use of a certain sort of language). Second, for many people for whom religion is salient it is not just one item among others that can be chosen; if a person is on the inside of a religion it may make a difference to many of the choices that she makes in her life.

If education is to help people find their way through the multiplicity of possibilities that face them in modern societies, the most obvious contribution it can make is to provide knowledge and understanding of the options available. Important though such knowledge and understanding is, what education can provide is limited, and perhaps not its most valuable contribution. Part of the reason for this is that a person now in school is likely (as life expectancy increases) to be living in a world of multiple possibilities for another 70 years or so: there is no possibility now of predicting all the choices that may open up, so that the capacity to gain new knowledge and understanding will be as important as anything that can be taught here and now about specific options. But more fundamental than knowledge about options is the question of whether people acquire an evaluative basis on which to make choices. As was pointed out in Chapter 3, no choice can be made without something being taken as a standard of evaluation; the idea of choosing all values at once is incoherent. But individuals can be perplexed about what standard of evaluation to follow if it seems that no standard is fixed and given. People need to be able to find their way, then, not just through a first-order array of options, but through the world of values which they can take into account when considering their options. That world in itself is inescapably plural (because not all values can be reduced to one common measure).

While some ways of acting will be ruled out by specific prohibitions or specific rights of others, most decisions in life are underdetermined by morality in the narrow sense. Possibilities of enjoyment, of satisfaction in achievement (which may call on effort that is not enjoyable in itself), of realisation of long-term rather than short-term goals, are only a few among the factors that may come into play. Education should help individuals, not just to be aware of the full range of considerations that may have a bearing on their decisions, but to have some reflective understanding of those considerations. This point, of course, has a bearing on the curriculum, to be considered below. Before that, I want to look at the ethical environment within schools.

The school environment

We saw in Chapter 1 that we may take the notions of school environment or classroom environment partly to refer to physical features of the environment, partly to social features. In the latter sense, the terms 'school ethos', 'school climate' and 'school culture' are already in use. For present purposes, without making the distinctions between those terms that may be relevant in empirical educational research,[1] we need only to notice the importance for values education of the ethical environment within the school. Simultaneously with opening up to children a sense of the range of choices that face them as individuals, schools will often give children their first experience of relationships outside their own family, so that much of their first learning about how to behave towards others who at least initially are strangers, about how to respond to perceived differences, and about how to cooperate in shared purposes, will take place within school. The quality of their experience within such an environment will clearly be important. That point could be accepted by people who may still have very different views about what kind of school environment is best for the learning of values. Often the direction of thought is that the way people relate to each other in the wider society should ideally exemplify certain values, and that the school environment should so far as possible act as a model for such social relationships. This direction of thought leaves room for people to differ in the values they emphasise. If justice in the wider society is the major concern, then perhaps what will be most important in the school is strict fairness in all dealings. If it is felt that in the wider society people have insufficient care and concern for each other, the desire may be for the school itself to be, above all, a caring community. If democracy is seen as central to the life of the wider society, perhaps the school should offer training for that, by itself being as democratic as possible. And so on.

That is not meant to suggest that schools cannot exemplify more than one value, only to recognise that attending to the quality of the ethical environment at the level of the school does not by itself determine what kind of environment that should be. But if the standards that were suggested earlier are accepted, we can try to apply them to the school environment. That environment should not be a psychologically unhealthy one, or one that anyone would feel excluded from even though they are formally members of the school. It should be sustainable, though perhaps the timescale over which sustainability is to be judged will be shorter than for a larger unit. A radical change in the ethical environment within a school may be possible and may be desirable if the previous environment has been unsatisfactory, but there may be difficulties in attempting to bring about changes too suddenly. The most important point for sustainability may be that where desirable changes are brought about, the means must be in place to maintain them. Superficial changes – a rewriting of a mission statement, a new rule about behaviour, an announcement of a new policy by the school principal – may not prove sustainable without deeper changes going on.

It is worth recalling here that while, in making decisions and arriving at judgements, it will sometimes be appropriate to follow general principles, we also recognise that persons can have desirable personal qualities – virtues – that are manifested in the way they respond to situations in which they find themselves, though often they will not be following principles at all. An institution such as a school can have virtues too. A school may be caring or uncaring, tolerant or intolerant, just or unjust, and so on. To ascribe such qualities to a school is not necessarily to refer to explicit principles that the school follows; it is to make an evaluation of the practices and procedures of the school. As in the case of individuals, there can be a discrepancy between the principles to which they subscribe and the qualities actually shown in their practice. A school may write 'respect' into a statement of its ethos but not display the virtue of respect for everyone within it.

What is necessary if a school is to display desirable qualities – the very qualities that it would wish its students to develop? It may not be essential that everyone working in the school has those qualities, as personal virtues, to a high degree, but it probably is necessary that all have a shared, even if a largely implicit, sense of the kind of place they want the school to be. That is, they will have some shared values, even if these are not explicitly spelled out as principles. It does not follow that in every school the same shared values should be uppermost; in other words, not every school has to be the same kind of ethical environment. We can apply to the ethical environment of a school a typology that Strike (2003) has used for possible kinds of educational community. One model for a community is a family, and some teachers will like to think of their school as a happy family. In such a school, affective interpersonal bonds of caring will be especially important (Noddings 1992). We may wonder how far such a model is possible for schools other than some small primary schools. Besides, a caring community is not necessarily united by any shared *educational* goals, just as a family does not necessarily have any shared goals, beyond getting along with each other (which may indeed be a valuable learning experience).

Another model of community, which Bottery (2004) places at the opposite end of a continuum, is the community as tribe. Strike's term 'tribe' is presumably meant to conjure up a picture of a small group who share almost everything in their way of life, have little privacy and little development of individuality: a strong and close-knit community. The members of it 'are the same in a deep way' (Strike 2003: 77). And as Strike points out, it scores very low on inclusiveness. Those who are not fully members of it are simply outsiders. We might add that those who are insiders tend to be members for life. This is hardly a realistic or desirable model for a school.

Strike's other two models of community do yield possible models for schools. One is a religious model, community as congregation. Its members constitute a community because they share certain beliefs or a certain world-view. The beliefs or worldviews in question are ones that are important across many areas of life, but at the same time they do not determine everything about how the members of a community live. A community that is constituted by the sharing of beliefs may be inclusive of a wide range of people and lifestyles, but cannot fully include people who do not share the beliefs. This is a possible model for a faith-based school. Whether there *should* be faith-based schools is a wider policy decision, which we shall come to below.

Next in Strike's scheme are shared practices. Members of an orchestra share in the practice of making music; this gives them a reason for cooperating *while they are functioning as an orchestra*. But outside of that context they may be quite different people with different beliefs and lifestyles. This is another possible model by which the members of a school could constitute a community: that they share a certain educational goal (a conception of what a good education is and the desire to achieve that) though they may not share a wider set of beliefs. This can be a viable metaphor for a secular school: a commitment to a shared conception of education incorporates a commitment to the values that are built into that conception or that are important to realising it.

But how values come to be shared can be important, as well as the fact that they are shared. A frequent theme in recent literature on educational leadership is that a school head or principal should have a vision for his or her school, and ensure that everyone else in the school comes to share it (cf. Sergiovanni 1994: 187–188). But the most one person can do is to influence an ethical environment, not create it from scratch. The leader who has a vision of what the school will be like, and who seeks to 'sell' it to the rest of the school, runs the risk of manipulation, of using the other members of the school as a means to realising her own dream. Or she may herself be only a channel through which a government is seeking to realise its own vision for education (Smith 2002). That terminology of 'vision' is often now part of the rhetoric of governmental education policy, even if it fits uneasily with the instrumentalism of much of the same policy.

A functioning community of shared values is more likely to be built from the bottom up. That may be a difficult and frustrating process, because it is unlikely to start with agreement on everything, and may never get to agreement on everything. But if we hope that the ethical environment within the school will be a model for the kind of ethical environment that would be desirable more generally, then a school in which people (including students as well as teachers) are constantly learning to cooperate on shared goals while living with disagreements may be a better model than one in which a sense of unity is imposed from the top.

The school system

Not everything that makes a difference to the ethical environment within a school can be determined at the level of the school itself. We have already noted that the idea that a school can be an educational community in which values are shared is liable to be realised in rather different ways in a secular or a faith-based school. But whether all schools in a society are to be secular and open to all, or all faith-based, or there is to be a mixture of the two, is the kind of structural feature of a school system that is usually determined at the level of government policy. It is by no means the only structural feature of a school system that may be relevant to the kind of ethical environment found within schools, but is perhaps especially pertinent because in some societies there is a public perception that faith schools make a stronger contribution to values education. Without getting into all of the factors that are relevant to policy (which would include, for instance, attitudes to private schooling and to state funding for schools that are not open to all), it is worth asking whether questions of policy on faith-based or common schools can be illuminated by considerations of the wider ethical environment. (I shall not take up at this point the question of possible differences in curriculum between the two kinds of school.)

Considerations of social cohesion, of inclusiveness within schools, and of the value of diversity, are all relevant. Chapter 4 argued for a rich environment across society in which there are not just many values but many kinds of values. We need different kinds of evaluative discourse so that all questions of evaluation are not reduced to one kind of consideration, be it cost–benefit analysis or any other unitary approach; that argument supported the inclusion of both religious and secular perspectives within the richness of the environment. But all the different values that make up a rich ethical environment are not just floating around unattached; values, as this book has assumed throughout, have to be located in persons, practices and institutions. And as we saw in Chapter 2, not all values can fit with all others. Despite a considerable human capacity for inconsistency, coherence sets some limits. The full extent of diversity that may be found within the environment cannot be attributed to any one individual. We should understand diversity of values, as a feature of the ethical environment, to imply diversity of people, that is, different people holding different values. And given the clustering of values that we considered in Chapter 2, induction into an ethical environment is always induction into some cultural context. We should not wish it to be otherwise, given the need for cultural coherence in the early years that was mentioned above. Putting these points together, we can say that a society in which there is to be diversity within the ethical environment has good reason, not just to uphold individualistic conditions that tend to encourage that diversity (such as freedom of association and of conscience) but also to uphold the possibility of different cultural identities coexisting.

Schooling, especially of relatively young children, is perhaps the major way outside the immediate family in which cultural identities can be either reinforced or (if the culture of the school is not supportive) undermined. So it appears that one way in which continuing diversity of ethical perspectives could be guaranteed is through society not just allowing but supporting the existence of schools rooted in different perspectives. Faith schools are the most obvious examples, though we should not forget the theoretical possibility of a variety of secular schools representing different perspectives, such as some devoted to the promotion of entrepreneurial activity and others to the protection of the natural environment. We can consider schools dedicated to particular value perspectives as examples of organisations other than government through which responsibility for the quality of the ethical environment can be exercised.

There is, then, an argument based on considerations of the ethical environment for the existence of a diversity of schools. The point here, however, is not to make a conclusive case either for or against such schools, but to point out the relevance of the environmental considerations. An appeal to those same considerations can also be used in an argument that favours common over separate schooling. The environmental argument is not simply for the right of each to be able to benefit from their own cultural membership (Kymlicka 1995), but for the benefits to all of the presence of perspectives other than their own. Those benefits will only accrue if there is contact between different perspectives. It might be suggested that all can be exposed to alternative perspectives simply through the operation of liberal institutions including free media within the wider society. Liberal practices, however, mean not only that there is freedom to disseminate views, but also that there is individual freedom to choose what to attend to and what to ignore. There is a possibility that those for whom initial cultural coherence has lasted right through their schooling will not have developed the disposition to listen to others. That is not to say they will have been indoctrinated, for they may retain the capacity to reflect on their beliefs and to be responsive to criticism when they take it seriously; the question is whether they will have the disposition to take alternative perspectives sufficiently seriously to exercise their critical capacity.

There is more to be said about what is involved in taking alternative perspectives seriously. We are not talking here about tolerance. Tolerance is insufficient and may be misplaced. In its origins, at least, even if not in common parlance today (Haydon 1997: 56), tolerance is a matter of putting up with something of which you disapprove. Where there is no disapproval, the question of tolerance does not arise. Perhaps we pride ourselves on our tolerance towards perspectives different from our own (which are not necessarily beliefs about right and wrong, but may be different conceptions of what matters in life). But if we are merely acknowledging that those perspectives are different, then given that mere difference does not give us any reason to disapprove, tolerance is misplaced.

Tolerance is often insufficient because it falls short of full recognition of and respect for the other. In liberal societies in recent years a common tendency, and ongoing demand, in matters for instance of sexual orientation, has been away from disapproval towards full recognition. This seems to be the right direction of change if the ethical environment is to meet the standard of inclusiveness, where that is taken to mean, as indicated in Chapter 4, not that all first-order views can be equally put into practice, but that all persons can feel themselves to have a stake in the ethical environment.

The move beyond tolerance to recognition requires understanding of the other (because we cannot otherwise know whom it is we are recognising), and that can best – perhaps only – come about through actual contact and dialogue between people whose value perspectives are different. In the ethical environment beyond the school we might hope for an atmosphere in which beliefs and commitments that are not mainstream can enter into public discourse rather than being treated as matters purely of private preference; but that wider culture of dialogue is unlikely to come about if it is not encouraged within schools (Haydon 1995; 2000c). So the aspiration towards an ethical environment that is both diverse and inclusive offers a strong argument for common schools in which people from many backgrounds mix. On the basis of argument independently of empirical evidence it may not be possible to go much further. Yet any actual evidence, as I shall mention in the Conclusion, will by its nature be far from conclusive. In those circumstances, a school system in which both separate and common schools exist may be the best that can be justified as a matter of public policy.

Values education in the school curriculum

On questions of the school curriculum in relation to values education it is difficult to make any empirical generalisations. The degree of public control over the curriculum (which may be at national or sub-national level) is much greater in some countries than in others. Where there is some centralised control, curricular requirements can be quite rapidly changed with changes of government or of policy. There may or may not be a requirement for specific programmes of instruction that have a special concern for values, and where there are such programmes they may go under very different labels: moral education, social education, personal education (and various combinations of these), ethics, social ethics, civics, citizenship are just a few. There is clearly great scope for variation in the content included under such labels. And where there are no such named programmes, this does not mean that there is no expectation that values education will be pursued in some way.

The primary point here is to consider what range of learning the school curriculum needs to make available to young people if they are to be able to find their way through the ethical environment, as well as to share in responsibility for its quality. How that range of learning is to be divided between different named areas of the curriculum is logically a secondary issue, though not trivial since the naming of curriculum areas can itself carry a certain message. Different conceptions of morality, for instance, may be conveyed if the idea of morality is seen as falling under religious education or under citizenship. But values education should in any case be treated as broader than an induction into morality.[2] If we understand the scope of values *education* by reference to the scope of the ethical environment, then we can say that anything that is to do with the ethical environment will come within the purview of values education (the open-endedness of this is not necessarily a problem, as it gives some scope to teachers' professional judgement about what is relevant for values education).

Since part of what education needs to do is to prepare people to face the range of decisions that contemporary societies demand, there is a sense in which everything in the curriculum is a part of values education. Within the context of compulsory schooling, the fact that something is in the curriculum at all (even as an option) presupposes that studying it can have some value, and no teaching in that context can be value-neutral. The point was made in the last chapter, *pace* Brighouse, that not even the teaching of Latin, let alone the facilitating of autonomy, could be value-neutral.

While there will be nothing in a curriculum that is not relevant to values education, we can still recognise that certain areas of the curriculum will have specific kinds of concern with values. We should not neglect aesthetic values. Though it might seem obvious from the name that 'values education' would include aesthetic values, in fact the term tends to be confined, if not to moral education narrowly, then to ethical values in the broad sense used in this book. But those who are responsible for values education in this sense ought at least to ensure that some attention is paid to the development of aesthetic appreciation, since the capacity to derive pleasure or a sense of meaning from art or from natural beauty can be an enrichment of life. Literature may have an especially important role, since it not only invokes aesthetic appreciation but also, as noted in Chapter 3, can provide access through imagination to a wider range of experience than that which the individual can gain at first hand. And the teaching of fiction can encourage explicit attention to the nature of the ethical environment within which a narrative is set.

Explicit attention to the ethical environment needs to be built into the curriculum, if that environment is not to be experienced just as part of the given context within which individuals live. History can have a role here, in showing how ethical environments have changed. And many branches of the social sciences are relevant, though in many countries such studies have not figured strongly in school curricula.

There are problems, though, in trying to build enough attention to issues about values into the learning of subjects that also have quite other grounds for their place in the curriculum. Certain areas of the curriculum may seem to have special concerns with values. One is citizenship; another, in countries in which it figures in the curriculum of publicly-funded schooling at all, is the study of religion. Neither of those can do all that needs to be done in values education; each has its own more specific concerns.

Religion in the ethical environment

The association of morality with religion has a long history, especially within the monotheistic religions in which it is possible to interpret moral demands as god-given law. In Western moral philosophy in recent centuries the tide has swung strongly towards the position that morality is logically independent of religion. This position does not claim that religious belief makes no difference to the morality of a believer; only that the possibility of having and using standards of right and wrong, good and bad, does not presuppose the existence of divinity. The recent tendency away from a law-like conception of morality towards virtue ethics can be construed as a move away from the kind of morality that arguably (Anscombe 1958) presupposes a divine law-giver towards a conception that seems at home in a naturalistic account of the human condition.

The recognition of arguments for the independence of morality from religion is important for secular schools, since it means that they can quite legitimately be concerned with morality without violating their secular nature. But it does not mean that such schools should pay no attention at all to the relationship between morality and religion (and there certainly are relationships of various kinds, even if they are not ones of logical implication). There are several reasons for not excluding the study of religion (as distinct from the transmission of a religious faith) from secular schools. One is that individuals should have the opportunity to consider for themselves what connections there may be between religion and morality. A second reason, not specifically connected with morality in the narrow sense, is the sheer importance of religious claims, *if* they are true. If part of the task of education is to help individuals find their way through the ethical environment, there is a case, even within a secular school system, not for promoting religious belief, but for making sure that no one is unaware of the claims of religion, so that everyone can look into those claims further if they wish.

Those are, of course, rather abstract arguments as presented here. What is to be made of them in practice will depend heavily on how far religion is a presence within the life of a particular society and on what is politically feasible. If religion is widely present within a society it may be politically easier for it to maintain a hold in schools; but the educational argument might well run the opposite way: the more that religion is an obvious presence within the wider society, the less need there will be for schools to draw attention to it. What is politically feasible will depend not just on statistical facts about the prevalence of religious belief but also on cultural understandings of the place of religion within a particular society (the differences in attitudes towards religion within the publicly-funded school systems of England, the USA, and France are cases in point).

Arguments for including within the curriculum some learning about religion fall far short of demonstrating that the study of religion could cover the whole field of values education. Any religious belief and set of practices will leave some of life's questions underdetermined. Even *if* religion gives answers to the most fundamental questions, it may be far from giving answers to many questions that still have to be answered, even if they are of lesser importance within a large view. These can include both personal choices within the day-to-day life of individuals, and, within the purview of citizens, questions of public policy, on which there is rarely unanimity between adherents of the same religion.

There is a different argument, however, relating not to the decisions facing individuals but to the quality of the ethical environment itself, which should have force in any society. This is the desirability of mutual understanding between those who have religious and those who have a-religious worldviews. That is an argument for the study of religion within secular schools but also for the study of secular outlooks within faith-based schools (Haydon 1994). This promotion of mutual understanding could well be considered an element of education for citizenship.

Education for citizenship

Does education for citizenship have a good claim to be considered as the primary vehicle for values education? Perhaps within some traditions of thought the good citizen is equated with a good person *per se*, so that there is at least a close link between citizenship and morality (Haydon 2000d). This interpretation is possible if by 'citizen' is meant 'member of society'; then citizenship will come close to encompassing the whole of the morality that applies to the dealings of persons with each other. But within a liberal way of thinking, where there is always some distinction to be made between the private and the public (though where the line should be drawn is controversial), there are close relationships between persons that call on different moral considerations from relationships between 'members of society' as such. Even if being a good parent is to be counted as part of being a good member of society – on the grounds that parenting is the bringing up of a citizen – it would be hard to bring all moral aspects of the parent–child relationship, or of other personal relationships, within the scope of citizenship. It is still less plausible to see citizenship education as covering, not just morality in the narrow sense, but the whole field of values.

Clarity in practice is likely to be promoted by recognising certain distinctive tasks for citizenship education. It is commonly said that social cohesion within any society requires some sharing of values (this is not, of course, incompatible with considerable diversity in other respects). Minimally, it requires some shared, if thin, conception of morality in the narrow sense. Explicit attempts within schooling to promote the adherence of all to a certain set of common values could well be, and often are, counted as one of the ways in which schools contribute to the basis of citizenship. But arguably the education of citizens should go further than simply presenting a set of values which it is hoped that citizens will assimilate. Within a democratic society students should be made aware of the basis for the selection of the favoured values. There are in principle several ways in which a favoured selection could be arrived at. It may be achieved through philosophical argument that tries to identify principles or civic virtues (Macedo 1990; Galston 1991; White 1996) that are essential to citizenship rather than representative of particular conceptions of the good life. It may be done through an attempt to draw out what is already implicit in the traditional understandings of citizenship within a particular society. It may be done through empirical methods (social surveys and the like) that attempt to find out what values actually are widely shared in a particular society. It may well be achieved through a combination of these ways. In any case it seems more congruent with democratic values that citizens (including young citizens) should not be purely passive in relation to whatever set of values the curriculum seeks to promote as shared values.

The discussion in Chapter 3 of a variety of conceptions of values education would suggest that the mere exposure of students to the statement of a set of values – whether as a set of principles or a set of named virtues – is likely to have little effect on the moral development of individuals. But we can see statements of shared values within an educational context as having a different function: to provide shared reference points for public discourse (Haydon 1999: 111). Even though the ostensibly shared values may be open to interpretation in significantly different ways, the existence of these reference points reduces the likelihood of citizens talking completely at cross purposes, since they will at least have a shared vocabulary by which to identify their differences. This will be important when controversial moral issues (of which abortion, genetic engineering, penal policy, animal experimentation, policy on immigration are just a few examples) need to be addressed through democratic processes.

The discussion in Chapter 5 points to another contribution that citizenship education can make. If citizens are not to be subject to manipulation, and are to be able to take a share in responsibility for their ethical environment, they need an understanding of the ways in which the ethical environment is formed. They need to know that governments and commercial organisations have ways open to them in which, whether intentionally or not, the ethical environment may be influenced without transparency. While citizenship education *could* try to see that citizens have this understanding, the government of the day will not necessarily want teachers to alert students to the ways in which government is influencing them. Teachers may nevertheless be able to take on this responsibility themselves.

Programmes of citizenship education are often designed *primarily* to promote the practice of citizenship within national boundaries. Some would argue that this is where citizenship properly belongs. The argument in brief would be that the practice of citizenship requires both shared bonds with fellow citizens and the existence of institutions through which the rights of citizens can be realised and their responsibilities carried out (Miller 2000). For historical reasons the relevant institutions operate mainly at the level of nation states, and psychologically the idea of nationhood seems able to function as a focus for identification with others. On such an argument the idea of global citizenship is at best metaphorical.

There is a strong argument on the other side, resting in the dangers of the nation state being both the locus of the institutions of citizenship and the focus of identity and loyalty. While there is no logical necessity for shared 'national sentiment' to be linked with the kind of nationalism that sees a particular nation as being superior to and in rivalry with others (White 1996), in practice rivalry between nation states has led to much conflict. It is much better, on this argument, for people to see themselves as 'citizens of the world', 'global citizens', or 'cosmopolitan citizens' (Nussbaum 1996; Dower and Williams 2002). Yet the conception of global citizenship still faces the problem that it may seem not to amount to full citizenship while the institutions of governance and democracy are not in place.

There is a danger of sterile argument over whether global citizenship is a genuine version of citizenship. Whatever we say about the meaning of 'citizenship', we can recognise that there is a global ethical environment within which local variations co-exist. Schools should certainly direct the attention of their students not only to their local or national ethical environment but to the global environment. How far this happens under the heading of citizenship is a secondary issue; in fact much of the knowledge about the wider world that is necessary is likely to come through other areas of curriculum including history and geography, as well as economics and politics if these are on the curriculum at all. A broader knowledge base brings with it the possibility of appreciating the richness and complexity of the ethical environment on a global scale. Young people can learn about important differences in ethical outlooks and also about shared concerns and about the elements of ethical and political discourse, including the language of human rights, which have worldwide currency. And they can come to recognise that issues of justice between individuals cannot be confined within national boundaries.

Education for citizenship, then, rightly has a large role to play within values education. But it should not be expected to occupy the whole field. Although it should provide young people with the knowledge and skills to enable them to play an active role in public affairs, and to give them a sense of their responsibilities as citizens, it cannot by itself settle for individuals just how much of their attentions and energies should be spent on engagement in public affairs.

The need for a synoptic view

Any life, especially within the complexity of modern conditions, has to achieve – or may, regrettably, fail to achieve – some balance between many different considerations. Even if each individual had in mind only their own satisfaction and happiness in life, the path would be far from easy. But the environment that individuals encounter will – quite properly – contain other kinds of consideration as well: some may present themselves as impersonal moral demands, some as matters of loyalty to friends and family, some as matters of national solidarity, some as obligations voluntarily entered into, and so on.

An education that aims to help people find their way through the complexities and demands of the ethical environment needs to give them ample space for reflection on the elements of that environment. Much of that reflection may be best pursued in conjunction with others, through dialogue about shared problems and challenges, since there is a shared ethical environment, though what is most salient within it may differ from one individual to another. Explicit attention to the contours of the ethical environment will not by itself deliver solutions to problems facing individuals, but educationally it should be a prerequisite. In many existing curricula it is hard to see where space will be found for such reflection.[3] Since the kind of understanding and reflection that is needed is essentially philosophical, there is a case for building some form of philosophy into the curriculum: the kind of dialogic practice that is often advocated by practitioners of philosophy for children rather than the academic study of philosophical texts.

In addition to space within the formal curriculum to learn about and reflect on the complexities of the ethical environment, there is a need too for young people to be able to talk both to each other and to caring and sensitive adults about individual problems. What is sometimes called the pastoral curriculum has to be complemented by pastoral care. That is one reason for giving attention, as we have, to the internal ethical environment of the school as well as to the curriculum.

The interaction between education and the ethical environment has been the theme throughout this book. What this chapter has attempted to illustrate is that there is no aspect of educational policy and practice that cannot be involved in that interaction. If we were to take that point seriously, none of our decision-making about education, whether at the level of national policy, internal school organisation or curriculum, would ignore the ethical environment.

Conclusion

In the final chapter I considered ways in which schools can help individuals to find their way through the complexities of the ethical environment. It is not only individuals who have to do this. So do families, communities and nation states themselves, within an ethical environment that in its totality is global. At all these levels the necessity to find a satisfactory way through the expectations, constraints and desirable goals that present themselves goes with a share in the responsibility for the ongoing quality of the ethical environment. The responsibility that starts with individuals extends through all those levels of collective life and collective decision-making in which individuals engage. So it would be possible to look at the responsibilities, not just of individuals in many roles, and not just of schools, but of organisations of many kinds including religious institutions, charities, local government and national government. In conclusion I shall draw attention to just a few of these levels of responsibility.

All, as citizens, can take a view on the quality of the ethical environment they find around them, and can work through whatever channels are available – which in a plural and democratic society will be many – for policies that will help to enhance that quality. At present, such a responsibility is not one that most people explicitly see themselves as having. That is one reason for values education, and citizenship education within that, to direct attention towards the ethical environment and towards the factors in government, commerce and public life that have a bearing on it. There can be no fixed list of what these factors are. At the end of Chapter 1 we looked at claims that the environment of certain societies is characterised by a sexist culture, a culture of violence or a culture of commercialism; further examples would not be difficult to find. Students in schools should be asked to scrutinise such claims so that they can continue as adult citizens to reflect on the nature of their ethical environment and their responsibility for it.

Parents, of course, have a responsibility for their own children's upbringing, but as I argued in the last chapter parents cannot reasonably be expected to take on the whole responsibility for enabling their children to understand and find their way through the ethical environment. Teachers have a responsibility that is complementary to that of parents rather than competing with it. A teacher cannot have the holistic responsibility for a child's ethical development that we may see parents as having. The teacher cannot be held responsible – in the sense of blameworthy – if particular individuals fail to develop the virtues society might wish them to develop, or fail to live up to the standards of other people's expectations. We can see teachers instead – and teachers can see themselves – as having a responsibility, shared with many others, for helping to sustain an ethical environment that makes it, on balance, more likely that individuals within that environment will live good lives. That responsibility is not to be fulfilled simply by 'delivering' a curriculum in values education that has been laid down by government. Since it is hard to say in advance what factors that come up in the environment of a school or in the content of a lesson may turn out to be relevant to gaining insight into the wider ethical environment, teachers need to have scope to exercise their professional judgement.

Academics researching into education also have channels through which they can help to support a healthy ethical environment. I hope, of course, that I have made some contribution by encouraging readers of this book to think about the ethical environment, but what I can say from a philosophical perspective is necessarily at a certain level of abstraction from concrete and local circumstances. In principle, many of the relevant questions about the factors that affect the ethical environment are empirical ones, yet they are ones that no realistic programme of research could conclusively settle. One would like to know what would be the effects across a whole society of the implementation of this or that school policy – such as state support for faith schools as against insistence on common schools for all – over, say, the next 30 to 50 years. The long time scale is desirable because we are talking about influences on the young, and we are interested in the nature of the society that they will partly constitute in future. But there is no empirical way of comparing one condition of a whole society with another, incompatible, condition of the same society. Nevertheless, much illumination can be brought by well-designed while necessarily more piecemeal research on, for instance, school climate and curriculum innovation. Such research should feed into public deliberation. The actual decisions that do make a difference to the ethical environment will often in the end be based not so much on evidence as on arguments of principle, which can be contested not just among academics but by the public in general.

Governments have large responsibilities in relation to the ethical environment. I have given in Chapter 4 examples of the way that legislation can have a positive effect on the ethical environment. The implementation of educational measures at a national level can also potentially have a positive and far-reaching effect. But I have stressed in Chapter 5 that this is by no means an argument for leaving it to governments to manipulate the ethical environment as they see fit. Citizens need to take their responsibilities seriously too.

The responsibilities of national governments cannot in a globalised world be confined within their own boundaries. In the case of the physical environment we are aware of how limited the powers of single governments are, if they cannot work in conjunction with other governments. In relation to the ethical environment as well, there is an important role for international cooperation. The Universal Declaration of Human Rights and a number of subsequent international agreements on rights (surveyed by Osler and Starkey 1996 in an educational context) are already important achievements, but there is clearly much more to be done before the aspirations of those agreements are fully met. The international aim for education should not be a standard model for values education in every school in every country: there are far too many local variations in the ethical environment that have to be taken into account. But that does not rule out some common features being introduced into values education across many countries through international agreements. The aim of these should be both to build shared understanding of features that are common across the global ethical environment, and to enable students to see the value of diversity

Not all features of globalisation have had positive results for values education. We have several times in this book noted the ethical climate brought into education by marketisation and its associated models of target-setting and accountability – tendencies that owe much to global forces (Bottery 2004). Governments and their policy makers need to be aware of unintended consequences. Many teachers and school leaders do succeed, perhaps against the odds, in satisfying the more instrumentalist demands of government policy while also keeping their eye on the aims that really count within their schools (Gold et al 2003; Sergiovanni 2005), but some do not (Ball 1999, 2003). Values education is too important an aim to be seen as a peripheral matter to be fitted into the interstices of a school's business. Yet many government policies have led towards an ethical environment in which schools, and individual teachers within them, face tensions that may be irresolvable without great cost to the meeting of genuinely educational aims and to the integrity of teachers. Such an ethical environment is not a healthy one, and perhaps not sustainable over the long term. Governments *should* be giving priority to sustaining an ethical environment in which values education has the best possible chance of fulfilling its own important responsibilities.

Notes

1 The ethical environment

1 Blackburn's approach in this introductory work is consistent with his much fuller essay in philosophical ethics, *Ruling Passions* (1998). He argues for the importance of attending to the ethical environment (though not then in that terminology) at 1998: 30–31. However, if I am right in this book, Blackburn takes too narrow a view of educational concerns when he says of virtue ethics 'This is the part of ethics that concerns educators, trying to turn out people of the right sort' (1998: 28). In my view, all parts of ethics, every 'focus of attention' (1998: 30) should be of concern to educators.

2 Knowledge of these experiments has extended far beyond social psychology. For philosophical critiques of them see Patten (1977), Pigden and Gillet (1996). A reader of an earlier draft of this book suggested that the electric shock experiments are 'a bit old hat'. So they are, and the very fact that they are illustrates an important point: that a piece of academic research can itself penetrate our ethical environment. The social psychologists Lee Ross and Richard Nisbett found it plausible in the early 1990s to claim that 'most educated people in the Western world know' about this experiment, 'for Milgram's demonstrations have become part of our society's shared intellectual legacy' (Ross and Nisbett 1991: 55). To the extent that they are correct, we can say that awareness of Milgram's experiments is part of our ethical environment. It has become so because the experiments are referred to and discussed. Whenever they are cited, as in this book, or as in a BBC *Horizon* documentary in October 2005 about the psychology of suicide bombers, they will inevitably seem 'old hat' to some, but will become part of the knowledge of others for the first time.

3 Note that Ball here uses the term 'ethical environment'. Also relevant is Ball 1998 where he uses, in a similar way, the terms 'moral environment' and 'values environment'.

4 The notion of the moral compass is used by Kant (see Chapter 3 below) and in the literature of educational management by Fullan (2003: 19).

2 The diversity of the ethical environment

1 I have argued for the importance of morality in the narrow sense (while emphasising that it does not occupy the whole of ethics) in Haydon 1999. See also Williams 1985: 174–196, 1995; Taylor 1989, Scanlon 1998.

2 Attention to conceptions of the good life (sometimes, but not invariably, analysed in terms of individual well-being) or simply of 'the good' has become common within recent philosophy. From the 1980s (MacIntyre 1981; Williams 1985: Ch. 3; Griffin 1986) there was increasing recognition within moral philosophy of the importance of looking at the idea of a good life, not just at questions of right and wrong.

3 Perhaps the most prominent theme in recent political philosophy, since Rawls 1971, has been the working out of liberal conceptions of justice. The theme of the good life has also figured strongly in recent political philosophy, with communitarians (see Chapter 5 below, note 2) emphasising the importance of shared conceptions of the good life while liberals often argue for the state accommodating a variety of conceptions of the good life (Rawls 2001; Kymlicka 2002; Sterba 2002).

4 'Virtue ethics' by now has its own large literature, e.g. Crisp 1996, Hursthouse 1999. In the next chapter I shall say more about virtues, and recognise that from the perspective of social psychology a question can be raised about their reality.

5 I am grateful to an anonymous reader of my first proposal for this book for asking this. Presumably 'we' in the question refers to some indeterminate set of Western, English-speaking, well-educated and probably fairly liberal-minded people. The answer in outline is that we do not have to tolerate *practices* that we sincerely judge to be *pernicious* (Concise Oxford Dictionary: destructive, ruinous, fatal) but that we ought to be very careful before labelling whole Cultures with that term.

3 Conceptions of values education

1 The idea that moral education is about teaching people *how* to think morally has been stressed especially by John Wilson (e.g. 1990) and also by Hare (e.g. 1992).

2 There is a position named particularism (Dancy 2004) which denies that we need ever give any role to general principles in judging what is to be done in specific situations.

3 In England the point was recognised in the work, and in the title, of the National Forum for Values in Education and the Community, set up in 1996 to see if agreement could be found on a set of common values. The list drawn up was later incorporated into National Curriculum documents. See Talbot and Tate 1997; Haydon 1998.

4 A recent example, which considers a range of earlier work, is Eisenberg 2004. Probably the earliest empirical study of cheating was by Hartshorne and May 1930.

5 These include Blackburn 1998: 36; Flanagan 1991: 293–314; Harman 2000: 165–178; within philosophy of education cf. McNamee 2002: 11–12.

4 Taking responsibility for the ethical environment

1 As mentioned in Chapter 1, the issue of whether and in what sense values can exist outside of human practices has been given recent attention by Raz and several respondents in Raz (2003).

2 That the causal effect has happened is a judgement of fact (presumably contestable, though I find it hard to see on what basis it could be contested). Whether the changes over time have on balance been for better or for worse is an evaluative judgement. I think on balance the improvements have outweighed the deteriorations; but that judgement about the past does not affect the point that we have a moral responsibility for what happens in the future.

3 The psychological health of those whose actions are constrained within a particular ethical environment cannot by itself be the only factor in evaluating that environment.

In some societies today perhaps the conduct that attracts more moral opprobrium than anything else is paedophilia. A climate of opinion that sometimes seems to tolerate almost anything else, but not that, no doubt creates psychological problems for a small minority of the population who are inclined towards paedophilia. That does not, by itself, do anything to invalidate the moral prohibition on their conduct. Even if we confine ourselves to consequentialist considerations, the long-term health, psychological and physical, of the abused must be a major factor.

4 I am using the term 'a-religious' here as a less misleading alternative to 'secular'. Where individual worldviews are concerned, a secular view will be one that does not incorporate or rest on any specifically religious concepts or beliefs, and will thus be equivalent to 'a-religious'. When it is state or educational policy that is in question, a secular policy is, similarly, one that does not incorporate or depend on specifically religious concepts or beliefs. But different secular policies can differ in whether they attempt to keep certain areas of the public domain free of religion altogether (as in the French policy of excluding ostentatious symbols of religion from state schools) or allow religious elements in while seeking neutrality between religious and a-religious perspectives. To apply the term 'secular' to a whole ethical environment would carry a similar ambiguity. I have discussed differing conceptions of secularity in Haydon 1994.

5 Intervening in the ethical environment

1 In the phrase 'patterns of interpretation and evaluation' Brighouse is referring to G. A. Cohen's argument that principles of justice should apply not just to the main institutions of society, but to the prevailing ethos as well (Cohen 1997).

2 Mulhall and Swift 1996, and Kymlicka 2002: Ch. 6, offer wide-ranging surveys of the debate between liberals and communitarians. See also Chapter 2 above, note 3.

3 In the discussion below I shall refer to England rather than Britain or the United Kingdom, in recognition of differences in the legal and educational systems in different parts of the UK, and of the uncertain scope of the evidence base for claims about public opinion made in the Strategy Unit Report.

4 Mill might even have accepted the Strategy Unit's claim that 'a key role of the state is to encourage in us behaviour that is in our own best interests' (p. 60), provided, of course, this is no more than encouragement.

6 The responsibilities of values education

1 Glover and Coleman (2005) have made a case for treating 'climate', 'ethos' and 'culture' as different notions within educational research.
2 If we wish to differentiate moral education within the broader field of values education, the obvious strategy is to try to clarify the notion of morality. This strategy has been followed by a number of writers, perhaps most notably John Wilson (e.g. Wilson 1990). I differ from Wilson in having a different take on the notion of morality (Haydon 2000b), and in taking a pragmatic approach to the differentiation of 'moral education' within 'values education'. I do not believe there is one uniquely correct analysis of the concept of morality (to which moral education should correspond), but if the practice were widely adopted of delineating moral education by reference to morality in the narrow sense (Haydon 1999), within the wider field of values education, this could make for greater clarity within educational discourse and practice.
3 In the context of England and Wales I have argued in Haydon 2005 that this space should be found within Personal, Social and Health Education.

References

Ackerman, B. (1980) *Social Justice in the Liberal State*, New Haven, CT: Yale University Press.

Advisory Group on Citizenship (1998) *Education for Citizenship and the Teaching of Democracy in Schools*, London: Qualifications and Curriculum Authority.

Annas, J. (2003) 'Virtue ethics and social psychology', online www.phil. canterbury.ac.nz/apriori/number2/julia_annas1.pdf (accessed November 2005).

Anscombe, E. (1958) 'Modern moral philosophy', *Philosophy* **33**.

Baier, A. (1985) *Postures of the Mind*, London: Methuen.

Ball, S. (1998) 'Ethics, self interest and the market form in education', in A. Cribb (ed.) *Markets, Managers and Public Service? Professional Ethics in the New Welfare State*, Centre for Public Policy Research, Occasional Paper No. 1, London: King's College.

Ball, S. (2003) 'Education for profit and standards in education: the ethical role of markets and the private sector in state systems'. In J. Oelkers (ed.) *Futures of Education II: Essays from an Interdisciplinary Symposium*, Bern: Peter Lang.

Beauchamp, T. and Childress, J. (1989) *Principles of Biomedical Ethics*, Oxford: Oxford University Press.

Benedict, R. (1946) *The Chrysanthemum and the Sword: Patterns of Japanese Culture*, Boston, MA: Houghton Mifflin.

Benn, S. (1988) *A Theory of Freedom*, Cambridge: Cambridge University Press.

Berlin, I. (1990) *The Crooked Timber of Humanity*, H. Hardy (ed.) London: John Murray.

Berlin, I. (1997) *The Proper Study of Mankind*, H. Hardy and R. Hausheer (eds) London: Chatto and Windus.

Berlin, I. (2000) *The Power of Ideas*, H. Hardy (ed.) London: Chatto and Windus.

Blackburn, S. (1998) *Ruling Passions*, Oxford: Oxford University Press.

Blackburn, S. (2001) *Being Good: A Short Introduction to Ethics*, Oxford: Oxford University Press.

Bottery, M. (2004) *The Challenges of Educational Leadership: Values in a Globalised Age*, London: Paul Chapman.

Brighouse, H. (2000) *School Choice and Social Justice*, Oxford: Oxford University Press.

Brighouse, H. (2004) *Justice*, Cambridge: Polity.

Brighouse, H. (2006) *On Education*, London: Routledge.

Bunting, M. (2004) 'Family fortunes', *Guardian*, '2020' Part 3, 25 September.

Callender, L. (2004) *Kant and Education*, unpublished PhD thesis, University of London.

Carr, D. (2003) 'Character and moral choice in the cultivation of virtue', *Philosophy* **78**.

Carr, D. and Steutel, J. (eds) (1999) *Virtue Ethics and Moral Education*, London: Routledge.

Clark, S. R. L. (1993) *How to Think about the Earth: Philosophical and Theological Models for Ecology*, London: Mowbray.

Cohen, G. A. (1997) 'Where the action is: on the site of distributive justice', *Philosophy and Public Affairs* **26**.

Cooper, D. E. and Palmer, J. A. (1998) *Spirit of the Environment*, London: Routledge.

Crisp, R. (ed.) (1996) *How Should One Live? Essays on the Virtues*, Oxford: Oxford University Press.

Curren, R. (2000) *Aristotle on the Necessity of Public Education*, Lanham, MD: Rowman and Littlefield.

Dancy, J. (1992) 'Caring about justice', *Philosophy* **67**.

Dancy, J. (2004) *Ethics Without Principles*, Oxford: Oxford University Press.

Darley, J. and Batson, C. (1973) 'From Jerusalem to Jericho: a study of situational and dispositional variables in helping behaviour', *Journal of Personality and Social Psychology* **27**.

Davidson, J. and Rees-Mogg, W. (1999) *The Sovereign Individual*, New York: Touchstone.

Davies, N. (2000) 'Fiddling the figures to get the right results', *Guardian*, 11 July.

Devlin, P. (1965) *The Enforcement of Morals*, Oxford: Oxford University Press.

Dower, N. and Williams, J. (eds) (2002) *Global Citizenship: A Critical Reader*, Edinburgh: Edinburgh University Press.

Downie, R. and Telfer, E. (1969) *Respect for Persons*, London: Allen and Unwin.

Eisenberg, J. (2004) 'To cheat or not to cheat: effects of moral perspective and situational variables on students' attitudes', *Journal of Moral Education* **38**.

Fishkin, J. and Laslett P. (eds) (2003) *Debating Deliberative Democracy*, Oxford: Blackwell.

Flanagan, O. (1991) *Varieties of Moral Personality: Ethics and Psychological Realism*, Cambridge, MA: Harvard University Press.

Fullan, M. (2003) *The Moral Imperative of School Leadership*, Thousand Oaks, CA: Corwin Press.

Galston, W. (1991) *Liberal Purposes: Goods, Virtues and Duties in the Liberal State*, Cambridge: Cambridge University Press.

Gibbard, A. (1990) *Wise Choices, Apt Feelings: A Theory of Normative Judgement*, Cambridge, MA: Harvard University Press.

Gilbert, D. and Malone, P. (1995) 'The correspondence bias', *Psychological Bulletin* **117**.

Gilligan, C. (1982) *In a Different Voice: Psychological Theory and Women's Development*, Cambridge, MA: Harvard University Press.

Gladwell, M. (2001) *The Tipping Point: How Little Things Can Make a Big Difference*, London: Abacus.

Glover, D. and Coleman, M. (2005) 'School culture, climate and ethos: interchangeable or distinctive concepts?', *Journal of In-service Education* **31**.

Glover, J. (1999) *Humanity: A Moral History of the Twentieth Century*, London: Jonathan Cape.

Gold, A., Evans, J., Earley, P., Halpin, D. and Collarbone, P. (2003) 'Principled principals? Values-driven leadership: evidence from ten case studies of outstanding school leaders', *Educational Management and Administration* **31**.

Green, J. (2004) 'Managerial modes of accountability and practical knowledge: reclaiming the practical', *Educational Philosophy and Theory* **36**.

Griffin, J. (1986) *Well-being*, Oxford: Oxford University Press.

Gutmann, A. (1987) *Democratic Education*, Princeton, NJ: Princeton University Press.

Habermas, J. (1990) *Moral Consciousness and Communicative Action*, Cambridge: Polity.

Hare, R. M. (1981) *Moral Thinking*, Oxford: Oxford University Press.

Hare, R. M. (1992) *Essays on Religion and Education*, Oxford: Oxford University Press.

Hargreaves, A. (2003) *Teaching in the Knowledge Society*, Milton Keynes: Open University Press.

Harman, G. (2000) *Explaining Value*, Oxford: Oxford University Press.

Hart, H. L. A. (1963) *Law, Liberty and Morality*, Oxford: Oxford University Press.

Hartshorne, H. and May, M. (1930) *Studies in the Nature of Character*, New York: Macmillan.

Haydon, G. (1994) 'Conceptions of the secular in society, polity and schools', *Journal of Philosophy of Education* **28**.

Haydon, G. (1995) 'Thick or thin? The cognitive content of education in a plural democracy', *Journal of Moral Education* **24**.

Haydon, G. (1997) *Teaching about Values: A New Approach*, London: Cassell.

Haydon, G. (1998) 'Between the common and the differentiated: reflections on the work of the School Curriculum and Assessment Authority on values education', *The Curriculum Journal* **9**.

Haydon, G. (1999) *Values, Virtues and Violence: Education and the Public Understanding of Morality*, Oxford: Blackwell.

Haydon, G. (2000a) 'What scope is there for teaching moral reasoning?', in

R., Gardner, J. Cairns, and D. Lawton, (eds) *Education for Values*, London: Kogan Page.

Haydon, G. (2000b) 'John Wilson and the place of morality in schools', *Journal of Moral Education* **29**.

Haydon, G. (2000c) 'Discussion of values and the value of discussion', in M., Leicester, C., Modgil, and S. Modgil, (eds) *Education, Culture and Values*, Volume III: *Classroom Issues: Practice, Pedagogy and Curriculum*, London: Falmer.

Haydon, G. (2000d) 'The moral agenda of citizenship education', in D., Lawton, J. Cairns, and R. Gardner, (eds) *Education for Citizenship*, London: Continuum.

Haydon, G. (2003) 'Moral education', in R. Curren, (ed.) *A Companion to the Philosophy of Education*, Oxford: Blackwell.

Haydon, G. (2004) 'Values education: sustaining the ethical environment', *Journal of Moral Education* **33**.

Haydon, G. (2005) *The Importance of PSHE: A Philosophical and Policy Perspective on Personal, Social and Health Education*, London: Philosophy of Education Society of Great Britain.

Hill, A. (2005) 'New Children's Czar vows: I'll stamp out the bullies', *Observer* (London) 13 November: 10–11.

Hofstede, G. (1980) *Culture's Consequences*, Newbury Park: Sage.

Hofstede, G. (1991) *Cultures and Organisations*, London: HarperCollins.

Horvath, A. (1991) 'The practice of theory', in B. Spiecker and R. Straughan (eds) *Freedom and Indoctrination in Education*, London: Cassell.

Huntington, S. (2002) *The Clash of Civilizations and the Remaking of World Order*, London: Free Press.

Hursthouse, R. (1999) *On Virtue Ethics*, Oxford: Oxford University Press.

Jeffrey, B. and Woods, P. (1998) *Testing Teachers: The Effect of School Inspections on Primary Teachers*, London: Falmer.

Kant, I. (1785) *Groundwork of the Metaphysic of Morals*, translated in H. Paton (1948), *The Moral Law*, London: Hutchison.

Katayama, K. (2003) 'Is the virtue approach to moral education viable in a plural society?', *Journal of Philosophy of Education* **37**.

Katz, M., Noddings, N. and Strike, K. (1999) *Justice and Caring: The Search for Common Ground in Education*, New York: Teachers College Press.

Kohlberg, L. (1981) *The Philosophy of Moral Development*, San Francisco, CA: Harper and Row.

Krakauer, J. (1997) *Into Thin Air*, London: Macmillan.

Kymlicka, W. (1995) *Multicultural Citizenship*, Oxford: Oxford University Press.

Kymlicka, W. (2002) *Contemporary Political Philosophy*, second edition, Oxford: Oxford University Press.

Lovibond, S. (2002) *Ethical Formation*, Cambridge, MA: Harvard University Press.

Macedo, S. (1990) *Liberal Virtues: Citizenship, Virtues and Community*, Oxford: Oxford University Press.

MacIntyre, A. (1981) *After Virtue*, London: Duckworth.

MacIntyre, A. (1999) 'How to seem virtuous without really being so', in J. M. Halstead and T. H. McLaughlin (eds) *Education in Morality*, London: Routledge.

McLaughlin, T. H. (2005) 'The educative importance of ethos', *British Journal of Educational Studies* **53**.

McNamee, M. (2002) 'Whose ethics, which research?', in M. McNamee and D. Bridges (eds) *The Ethics of Educational Research*, Oxford: Blackwell.

Milgram, S. (1974) *Obedience to Authority*, London: Tavistock.

Mill, J. S. (1975) *On Liberty* (first published 1859), in J. S. Mill, *Three Essays*, Oxford: Oxford University Press.

Miller, D. (2000) 'Bounded citizenship', in Miller, D. (ed.) *Citizenship and National Identity*, Cambridge: Polity.

Mirembe, R. and Davies, L. (2001) 'Is schooling a risk? Gender, power relations and school culture in Uganda', *Gender and Education* **13**.

Mulhall, S. and Swift, A. (1996) *Liberals and Communitarians*, second edition, Oxford: Blackwell.

Noddings, N. (1984) *Caring: A Feminine Approach to Ethics and Moral Education*, Berkeley, CA: University of California Press.

Noddings, N. (1992) *The Challenge to Care in Schools: An Alternative Approach to Education*, NewYork: Teachers College Press.

Nussbaum, M. (1996) 'Patriotism and Cosmopolitanism', in M. Nussbaum (ed. J. Cohen) *For Love of Country*, New York: Beacon Press.

Osler, A. and Starkey, H. (1996) *Teacher Education and Human Rights*, London: David Fulton.

Patten, S. (1977) 'Milgram's shocking experiments', *Philosophy* **52**.

Pigden, C. and Gillet, G. (1996) 'Milgram, method and morality', *Journal of Applied Philosophy* **13**.

Popper, K. (1972) *Objective Knowledge: An Evolutionary Approach*, Oxford: Oxford University Press.

Prime Minister's Strategy Unit (2004) *Personal Responsibility and Changing Behaviour: The State of Knowledge and its Implications for Public Policy*, online www.strategy.gov.uk/files/pdf/pr.pdf (accessed 17 February 2005).

Prosser, J. (ed.) (1999) *School Culture*, London: Paul Chapman.

Rawls, J. (1971) *A Theory of Justice*, Oxford: Oxford University Press.

Rawls, J. (2001) *Justice as Fairness: A Restatement*, Cambridge, MA: Harvard University Press.

Raz, J. (1986) *The Morality of Freedom*, Oxford: Oxford University Press.

Raz, J. (2003) *The Practice of Value*, Oxford: Oxford University Press.

Riggs, J. and Gumbrecht, L. (2005) 'Correspondence bias and American sentiment in the wake of September 11, 2001', *Journal of Applied Social Psychology* **35**, 1.

Ross, L. and Nisbett, R. (1991) *The Person and the Situation*, Philadelphia, PA: Temple University Press.

Rustin, M. (1997) 'Innate morality: a psychoanalytic approach to moral education', in R. Smith and P. Standish (eds) *Teaching Right and Wrong: Moral Education in the Balance*, Stoke on Trent: Trentham.

Scanlon, T. (1998) *What we Owe to Each Other*, Cambridge, MA: Harvard University Press.

Schor, J. (2004) *Born to Buy*, New York: Scribner.

Schumpeter, J. (1950) *Capitalism, Socialism and Democracy*, third edition, London: Allen and Unwin.

Schwartz, B. (2004) *The Paradox of Choice: Why More Means Less*, New York: HarperCollins.

Sergiovanni, T. (1994) *Building Community in Schools*, San Francisco, CA: Jossey-Bass.

Sergiovanni, T. (2005) *Strengthening the Heartbeat: Leading and Learning Together in Schools*, San Francisco, CA: Jossey-Bass.

Smith, M. (2002) 'The School leadership initiative: an ethically flawed project?', *Journal of Philosophy of Education* 36.

Smith, P. and Bond, M. (1993) *Social Psychology across Cultures*, Hemel Hempstead: Harvester Wheatsheaf.

Smith, R. (1997) 'Judgement day', in R. Smith and P. Standish (eds) *Teaching Right and Wrong: Moral Education in the Balance*, Stoke on Trent: Trentham.

Smith, R. (2003) 'Teaching literature', in R. Curren (ed.) *A Companion to the Philosophy of Education*, Oxford: Blackwell.

Snook, I. (ed.) (1972) *Concepts of Indoctrination*, London: Routledge.

Sterba, J. (2002) 'Liberalism and the challenge of communitarianism', in R. Simon (ed.) *The Blackwell Guide to Social and Political Philosophy*, Oxford: Blackwell.

Strike, K. (2003) 'Community, coherence and inclusiveness', in P. Begley and O. Johansson (eds) *The Ethical Dimensions of School Leadership*, Dordrecht: Kluwer.

Talbot, M. and Tate, N. (1997) 'Shared values in a pluralist society?', in R. Smith and P. Standish (eds) *Teaching Right and Wrong: Moral Education in the Balance*, Stoke on Trent: Trentham.

Taylor, C. (1989) *Sources of the Self*, Cambridge: Cambridge University Press.

Turnbull, C. (1974) *The Mountain People*, London: Pan.

Waldron, J. (1996) 'Multiculturalism and melange', in R. K. Fullinwider (ed.) *Public Education in a Multicultural Society*, Cambridge: Cambridge University Press.

Warnock, M. (1977) *Schools of Thought*, London: Faber.

White, J. (1990) *Education and the Good Life*, London: Kogan Page.

White, J. (1991) 'The justification of autonomy as an educational aim', in B. Spiecker and R. Straughan (eds) *Freedom and Indoctrination in Education*, London: Cassell.

White, J. (1996) 'Education and nationality', *Journal of Philosophy of Education* **30**.

White, J. (2002) 'New light on personal well-being', *Journal of Philosophy of Education* **36**.

White, P. (1996) *Civic Virtues and Public Schooling: Educating Citizens for a Democratic Society*, New York: Teachers College Press.

Williams, B. (1985) *Ethics and the Limits of Philosophy*, London: Fontana.

Williams, B. (1995) 'Moral luck: a postscript', in B. Williams (ed.) *Making Sense of Humanity*, Cambridge: Cambridge University Press.

Wilson, J. (1990) *A New Introduction to Moral Education*, London: Cassell.

Wittgenstein, L. (1972) *Philosophical Investigations*, Oxford: Blackwell.

Index

References to certain kinds of idea, reason, consideration etc. – such as aesthetic, instrumental, spiritual, – are listed under 'values'.